Erin Pizzey founded Chiswick Wo
in 1971. Landmarks in her career c
officialdom in defence of women and children have included an
appearance at the House of Lords and the publication in 1974 of
the influential *Scream Quietly or the Neighbours will Hear*. Her
autobiography, *Infernal Child*, was published in 1978. She now
writes regularly for *Cosmopolitan*.

Also by Erin Pizzey

INFERNAL CHILD

Erin Pizzey

THE SLUT'S COOK BOOK

Illustrations by Anny White

Futura
Macdonald & Co
London & Sydney

A Futura Book

First published in Great Britain in 1981 by
Macdonald & Co (Publishers) Ltd
First Futura edition 1982

ISBN: 0 7088 2214 2

Printed in Great Britain by
Richard Clay (The Chaucer Press) Ltd,
Bungay, Suffolk

Futura Publications
A division of Macdonald & Co (Publishers) Ltd
Maxwell House
74 Worship Street
London EC2A 2EN

To my Bagel
with love,
Blintz

CONTENTS

Note
All recipes in this book are designed to serve 6 people unless otherwise stated.

as she glides up the stairs, the SLUT looks at her kitchen

INTRODUCTION

I am writing this cookbook as a result of twenty years of rage and frustration at my inability to live up to anyone's idea of a good cook, never mind a hostess. If I was entertaining in my home I was usually so tired by the time I'd scraped the children off the wall and thrown them into bed that the thought of an obligatory three-course meal nauseated me. The making of it raised my blood-pressure. The serving of it made me hate the guests, so I usually left the table and the startled guests at about half-past ten. I was married at the time. Before we divorced we had few guests. Maybe that was because when we were guests in their homes, and I couldn't put myself to bed at half-past ten, I would get drunk and disorderly and would have to be removed by my patient husband.

I have attended one dinner party since my divorce. Nothing has changed. We were served a three-course meal. The hostess dithered, flustered, popped out of the room to shriek at the children and returned to apologize for the food yet again. So she should. It was awful. But I had changed. I had learned the art of being a 'slut'.

A slut is a much maligned human being. It is usually quite wrong to assume that a slut is promiscuous – nothing is further from the truth. A slut is always in control of every situation she is in. She therefore only involves herself in relationships of her own choice. It is, alas, her poor sister the 'slag' who has given the slut a bad name. Both in her kitchen and in her bedroom the slut calmly goes about her business of avoiding any taint of coercion from any source other than her own innate creativity. Within every woman there is a slut dying to get

9

out. But our bondage is such – thanks to television, advertising, and our need to compete with each other – that few women are prepared to take a stand. Sluts of the world unite! You have nothing to lose except your Valium.

This book looks at the slut's style of entertaining. It is written for those who get perverse pleasure out of expending very little energy for an awful lot of praise. If you are the sort of woman who needs callouses on your knees from scrubbing the floor, or beads of sweat on your brow from kneading dough, put this book down. Everyone else read on for a crash course in instant entertaining.

Sluts love people. They don't make friends with a view to business, or 'social' friends, since they are far too busy having a good time to waste it on idle chatter. A slut is always at risk when she tries to be anything other than herself because she usually gets bored and can then be horribly rude. Her house is full of people from all walks of life, and feeding them is one of her happiest pastimes. A slut is seldom very good at anything in particular except sensual pleasure. Food, therefore, comes high on her list. She cooks for pleasure and enjoys the result of fulfilled people round her table.

All sluts love the idea of machines: the concept of anything that will do arduous tasks on their behalf is irresistible. However, a slut is incapable of looking after or maintaining anything mechanical. Her kitchen will be fitted out with all sorts of gadgets, all of which at some time or another have exploded or caught fire and now sit there sullenly while she gets on with her cooking pots and a wooden spoon. Ideally, for perfect cooking, a slut should have a live-in lover to take the place of the machines, providing of course that she has made sure that he can maintain himself. Otherwise he is merely a liability and hangs out next to the machines.

The slut's best friend is a tin-opener. Of course, she will have an expensive tin-opener that sticks to the wall but is never used because she can't remember which way to put the tin in, so it usually ends up hungrily chewing the rim. She actually uses a metal opener from Woolies. The only other machine she constantly uses is a pressure-cooker. The pressure-cooker is a continual source of violence both

the SLUT'S BEST FRIEND
is a TiN OPENER

to herself and to her guests, but it cooks everything so fast and cuts work so dramatically that she wouldn't be without it. Also, it suits her perverse sense of humour to see her guests diving under the dinner table or escaping through windows as the cooker reaches its climax, hissing steam and dislike over everyone. The instruction book is always lost (sluts don't like other people's advice even if they risk their lives) so it's a gamble whether dinner will be excellent or will be plastered on the ceiling. If it is on the ceiling, she gets the guests plastered and then produces an alternative meal in twenty minutes. A good slut *never* takes more than twenty minutes' working time to produce a dish, and when disaster befalls her she always rises to the occasion magnificently.

In the kitchen a slut usually has a good-sized fridge which is always on the point of collapse because she never remembers to defrost it. Scavenging guests or lovers tend to get severe cases of frostbite. You can usually spot the live-in lover by the absence of a finger or two either from rummaging in the fridge or from trying to mend the hostile machines. The slut will, of course, have a freezer which is always empty because her food is so good that there are no leftovers. If there is anything in it, she never remembers to take it out in time for it to thaw. Occasionally she finds the freezer useful for sobering up an obstreperous guest – ten minutes inside with the lid locked has a wonderfully calming affect on the drunk in particular and on everyone in the house in general. It must be remembered that a slut's entertaining is so stimulating that she must have reserve methods of dealing with people who get over-excited lest everyone disappears under the table before the last course and gives her house a bad name.

The slut's cooker can be either gas or electric, old or new, because she only cooks at one temperature – the highest. The saucepans usually look good on the outside because she likes bright colours, but the inside closely resembles Hiroshima. The latest piece of equipment in every slut's kitchen is a micro-wave oven, because it cooks everything instantly. It is hardly used, of course, but it does provide the pleasure of watching a live-in lover walk around on stilts, as the micro is said to emit waves that

12

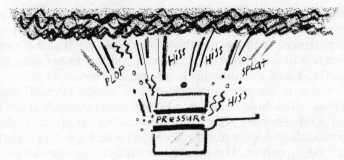

IF the DINNER IS ON the CEILING

she GETS the GUESTS PLASTERED

waft through men's trousers, thereby rendering them in-fertile. A thoughtful slut buys the stilts at Harrods' toy department with a matching tracksuit so that he can practise in the garden. It is a great comfort to her (and to him) to know that only his knees are infertile.

A slut is the enemy of housework. So the kitchen, and indeed the whole house, has huge fitted cupboards and no exposed shelves. Once the doors are shut, it looks immaculate. Never mind the chaos behind the doors; that can be forgotten. The house has built-in furniture every-where so there is no need to flush out generations of mice/shoes/knickers. The only free-standing furniture is big sofas and a large pine table that is stained with wine, garlic and olive oil. Round the table is a motley collection of wooden chairs that can withstand even the stoutest of guests. They all have arm-rests so that a good deal of talking can take place. The splaying of legs and the loosen-ing of belts is also contained in these chairs, as otherwise guests have a bad habit of splaying their legs, loosening their belts, and falling in a drunken stupor out of their chairs and on to their heads. If they scream, it disrupts the pleasure of satiety; if they stay silent, they might be dead and everyone else starts screaming. There is nothing more aggravating for a slut than to have to perform mouth-to-mouth resuscitation on a prostrate guest, unless of course she fancies him. This is hardly likely, because sluts are very cool ladies who like their men to be equally cool – falling on his head in a drunken stupor will not endear a man to a slut. She usually passes up the mouth-to-mouth in favour of a firm squeeze in the region of the prostate. If he opens his eyes in horror and makes choking noises, everyone gets back to dinner. If he remains silent he is obviously dead and goes into the freezer until after the washing-up (a chore always done by guests).

Sluts aren't interested in food during the day. They sleep most of the day anyway. When a slut is about to create her evening, she approaches it like a theatre produc-tion. Her friend is the grocer; her stage manager is her bank manager, who endlessly lets her overdraw because he understands that no self-respecting slut would be seen dead without an overdraft; the stage is peopled by her

friends who come to dinner. All of them are hungry for her food, her warmth, and for the business of the evening that lasts long into the night, when finally they stagger into the rising morning, full of happiness and fond memories. Those who can't stagger hail a passing policeman who obligingly arrests them. They sleep a few hours in the local police station, which is well used to providing the slut with extra accommodation, since some of the policemen also come to dinner.

As she glides up the stairs, the slut looks at her kitchen. 'Tomorrow is another day,' she thinks to herself and falls asleep, dreaming of aubergines, purple and hard, of green peppers full of spice and mince, of prawns at sea in whisky, of crabs and of salads. She sleeps, and cooks in her dreams.

15

ONE
STARTERS

FIRST COURSES
ARE designed to give
PEOPLE TIME TO RELAX +
get to KNOW
EACH OTHER

STARTERS

It is obviously ridiculous to prepare a first course that depends on split-second timing. Sluts are incapable of timing anyway, and their clocks never work. So rule number one is to prepare a first course that can cook for ever or that can sit on a plate without congealing or melting. The mounting sense of panic as people fail to arrive – or if they do arrive vaguely on time, refuse to come to the table – is not for us sluts. Of course, one can approach the dissenting guest with a hammer and give him no choice, but this tends to upset the tone of the evening, particularly if the other guests are squeamish.

Millionaire's Salad is a good starter, and it sounds expensive and exotic. Actually it is the heart of a palm tree – a fact you should avoid mentioning to any earnest conservationist who may be at the table, in case he has visions of night raids on the Palm House at Kew Gardens and refuses to sully his lips. The only snag with this recipe is the mayonnaise. Most people have their own method of making it. Sluts throw it all together and usually get it right. If they don't they throw it all out and reach for the Hellman's which they doctor with a little black pepper, 2 crushed cloves of garlic and some fresh lemon juice. Some people can't taste the difference. However, before giving up on the real stuff, it's worth trying several well-known tricks.

Millionaire's Salad with Mayonnaise

3 tins palm hearts	Salt to taste
2 eggs	1 large fresh lemon
½ pint olive oil	Black pepper to taste
1 tablespoon vinegar	

I allow two palm hearts on a plate for each person, and put the mayonnaise in a bowl on the table so that people who are addicted to it can make pigs of themselves.

Slut's Mayonnaise

It is perfectly possible to make excellent mayonnaise in a mixer, but I assume that my fellow sluts' mixers are either in the repair shop or are missing a vital part, so I will stick to a mixing bowl and a wooden spoon. Actually, as I am usually in a panic in case it doesn't work, I am liable to use anything that comes to hand. If you are a Catholic, it helps to begin with a word to St Jude (the patron saint of hopeless cases).

It is vital that you remember to take the eggs out of the fridge a good while in advance so that the oil and the eggs are the same temperature. However, as you are unlikely to have remembered until it's far too late, put the eggs in warm water for 10 minutes before you break them into a bowl.

Now, sit down comfortably. Mayonnaise is sneaky stuff and can sense a nervous beginner. If you don't feel confident, fill your glass with gin and take a deep slug.

Break the two egg yolks into a mixing basin, and beat them to death. Good housewives save the whites; sluts watch them slide gelatinously down the drain since the cats won't eat them. Alternatively, if you're feeling particularly ugly you can smear them on your face as a natural face-pack (don't forget to take it off before you greet the guests).

Crush 1 to 8 cloves of garlic, depending on your addiction to this beautiful vegetable. (Medical note: Garlic is good for everything from heart disease to keeping vampires away.)

Start to drip olive oil into the eggs. The problem is not to get so bored that you slosh the stuff into the bowl and everything curdles. It is at this point that you face the first test of whether it is going to work or not. It should, after twenty or thirty stirs with the spoon, thicken. If it doesn't, take action immediately. It's easier to correct it now than later, and also less expensive. If the room is very hot, sit the bowl on a bed of ice for the next 10 minutes to help the sauce emulsify. If the room is cold, add a tablespoonful of hot water to the mixture, which will have the same effect. If it is beginning to curdle, beat another egg yolk into it. (Don't spit into it. This is an old wives' tale and it really doesn't work.)

Assuming you've got this far and the mixture is thickening, drip vinegar into it slowly. I prefer malt vinegar, but people have their own ideas as to how it should taste, and there are endless types of wine vinegar – try them all.

Taste it and add salt and black pepper until it makes you happy. A lemon taste goes well with palm hearts, so squeeze a lemon into the bowl, and the mixture will turn from a rich egg yellow into a white, thick-looking cream.

Mayonnaise is like love: the more times you make it, the better it becomes.

Avocado Dip

Avocados are served by everyone. Unfortunately, they are usually filled with blotting-paper type prawns and a horrible pink sauce. They have such a delicate taste that they are far better left alone and served with a little oil and vinegar or as a dip. Try this one:

4 large or 6 small avocados	2 tablespoons Madras curry powder
1 small carton sour cream	1 box Melba toast

If you are mechanically minded, use a blender to purée the avocados; the rest of us will mash them up with a fork. Purists insist on a silver implement, but since any slut owning anything silver will find it dirty, use a wooden spoon. Once it is sufficiently mushy, squeeze in the juice of a lemon and add the sour cream. Now add salt and black pepper to taste, along with the Madras curry powder. Sluts tend to like everything fairly highly spiced, so it is a question of tasting the mixture until you are satisfied.

Cover the dip and keep it in the fridge until you are ready to serve; eat it with Melba toast. Baking your own toast is no problem, except that you require an alert mind in order to retrieve it from the oven before it turns into charcoal. If this happens, save it till the end of the meal, then hand it round with instructions to chew slowly as an aid to digestion. The guests will think this is the latest London fashion and will munch obediently.

Avocados and Red Bean Salad

4 large or 6 small avocados	1 tablespoon olive oil or walnut oil
1 tin red kidney beans	1 lemon
6 spring onions	Salt and pepper
1 clove garlic	Parsley

Mash the avocados. Drain the tin of red beans. Chop the spring onions, remembering that the strongest taste is in the green part. Split open the clove of garlic and look for the little shoot in the middle. (This is easier to see in certain types of garlic, but if you search hard you will find it even in the plain white cloves.) It is the shoot which has a bitter taste and retains the smell. This dish needs just a hint of garlic, so it is best to remove the shoot. Mix all the ingredients together with a tablespoon of fragrant French olive oil or, if you are feeling extravagant, walnut oil which has a lovely taste all of its own. Add the juice of half a lemon, and sprinkle it liberally with parsley. Serve with toast or French bread.

It is worth noting that parsley is a very efficient deodorant. If you are a garlic lush, keep pots of parsley in the garden and chew it furiously before you face the human race the next morning. Sluts tend to eat so much garlic that they become unaware of the smell. They thus enjoy buses and tubes all to themselves.

It all gets very
friendly + messy

Avocados and Caviar

4 large or 6 small
   avocados
12 petit Swiss cheeses
2 medium-sized jars of
   lumpfish roe

Black pepper
Lemon juice

It always seems a shame to throw away those lovely
avocado stones. You can tell a fellow slut by the number of
jars with stones balanced precariously on match-sticks, full
of slimy yellow water, littering her kitchen. Slags keep the
stones in a pile behind the front door to hurl at departing
lovers, while Hampstead Housewives paint them and give
them away as unwelcome Christmas presents.

Mix the cheese and the lumpfish roe. (Make sure you
drain the jars before decanting, otherwise it all gets too
wet.) If you are going to make this course well ahead of
time, which of course you should, sprinkle lemon juice
over the halves of avocados lest they go black and look like
the plague. Put large dollops of the mixture in the middle

22

of the avocado halves, and dust the whole thing with fresh black pepper.

Of course, there are people who can afford not just lumpfish roe but the real thing. If you are lucky enough to be given a tin of caviar, forget the guests and spend the money on a bottle of champagne (preferably Dom Perignon) and invite your loved one to your bedroom.

Caviar au Sensuel

1 tin caviar, begged, borrowed or stolen	2 large scented candles
	2 teaspoons
2 bright yellow, bursting lemons	1 cold bottle Dom Perignon champagne
Dry crunchy toast	2 champagne goblets
1 double bed	2 satisfied smiles
Satin sheets, brown, black or purple	1 locked door
	1 telephone off the hook

PS. If you have kids, bribe a friend to take them for the night.

Taramasalata

Taramasalata sounds so much nicer than 'fish eggs' or even 'cod's roe'. This delicious creamy dip can be made quite simply. All it takes is:

3 oz smoked cod's roe, preferably potted	1 liberal pinch cayenne pepper
2 slices crustless white bread, soaked in water and squeezed dry	About 6 oz corn or nut oil
	1 crushed clove garlic
	1 or 2 lemons

Pound the roe to a mush in a mortar (or use an electric blender).

Mix in the now soggy but squeezed bread. The bread can be a little stiff before soaking, but not too old. Add the garlic and pepper to taste.

Add the lemon juice and the oil bit by bit, stirring con-

stantly as for mayonnaise. Keep beating until the mixture
is the consistency of stiff mayonnaise.

If you don't have the time to make taramasalata (though
not much time is required) you can always buy some at the
local deli. This method is even quicker and easier, but
make sure the bought stuff isn't too old, in which case it
looks like axle grease. Sometimes it has been so cheaply
made that it is horribly watery. It's worth sticking your
finger in at the shop and tasting. If anyone from the Health
Department is looking, you can always pretend to be
rescuing a fly from imminent death as you are a Buddhist
and are devoted to saving life.

My local shop is Adamou's on Chiswick High Road. I
know the whole family of Adamous, who have put up
with me bravely for the last nine years. They are a Greek
Cypriot family who love food, and the place is stuffed with
everything from everywhere. Whenever the world becomes an alien place to inhabit (every Monday morning), I
disappear into the cave-like warmth of this shop and lose
myself among the mangoes and the melons. At the back
are mounds of green lettuces: cos, long and bitter; Webb's,
sweet and chewy; Icebergs, crisp and nutty. Bundles of
wild herbs and trays of different curries scent the sweet
air. If I'm lingering, I talk to Adam, who is the philo-
sopher, or to his mother about methods of cooking various
vegetables. I enquire about Naki's children or ask whether
Grandpa has lost any more pigeons. I buy some pitta bread
to serve with taramasalata, and, if I'm in the mood, decide
to pop down to Portch's, the wet-fish shop a little further
down the road, to buy some smoked cod's roe in its
natural casing.

The only problem with smoked cod's roe is that the
ovaries look very like large testicles; this tends to put
many people off, which is a shame because it is delicately
smoked and has a delightful taste. Sluts are very basic
people, however, and are not at all bothered by shapes,
sizes or smells.

Smoked Cod's Roe

1 large portion smoked cod's roe	Lemon juice Black pepper and salt

I shall refrain from calling the sac an ovary, in deference to my more squeamish readers, and shall henceforward refer to it as a 'portion'. The easiest way of serving this is to split it lengthwise and cut off the wrinkled end so that it doesn't look quite so anatomical. Put it on a dish and surround it with wedges of lemon, and have a peppermill handy. Let people spoon out the roe on to their own plates. If you feel that several guests are liable to spoil the first course, for they are pale green with their heads between their knees (and you are sure it's not just one of your promiscuous friends with her head between someone else's knees), there is a more palatable compromise available. Cut the roe into 2-inch slices and put it on individual plates where it looks more anonymous but adds to the washing-up. Serve it with toast or French bread. It's a rich course and very filling.

Tahina

Lots of people get put off by reading recipes for tahina that require hours of soaking chick peas and of banging away in general. A good slut, however, knows her local shops. You can find tins or jars of this delicious chick-pea paste called tahina in most delicatessens.

1 jar tahina	Juice of 2 large lemons
3 tablespoons olive oil	Black pepper and salt to
3 crushed cloves garlic	taste

Decant the tahina paste from the jar and add the crushed cloves of garlic. Beat in the olive oil and then add the lemon juice slowly. The paste usually takes the oil well but' threatens to have a nervous breakdown when attacked by the lemon juice. Don't worry. Just keep beating the mush. The lemons turn it from a horrible grey to a lovely, evenly white paste. Serve it with pitta bread or toast.

+RY WEARING
DARK GLASSES

If you like tahina, and most people do, this next recipe is even richer.

Baba Ghanoush (Aubergines with Tahina)

2 large aubergines	3 lemons
5 cloves garlic	A bunch of parsley
½ pint tahina	Salt and black pepper

To skin the aubergines, you can if you like follow the recommended method of charring them under the grill. Sluts don't have that kind of patience though, and usually end up with horribly burnt fingers. It is easier just to peel them and then fry them gently until they are soft. Then mash them with a wooden spoon or risk using the blender. Add the crushed garlic, salt and black pepper. Slowly add the tahina and then the lemon juice, beating the mixture very thoroughly until it is a rich creamy paste. Serve it with pitta bread, and decorate the bowl with sliced tomatoes, black olives and lemon wedges.

Crudités

This is a very good way to start dinner, particularly if people don't know each other very well. By the time they've dunked lots of different vegetables into the mayonnaise, it all gets very messy and friendly. Before long they are sucking their fingers, and then each other's. If things look as though they are going to degenerate even further, open some more wine, turn out the light and forget the rest of the meal. (It saves on the washing-up.)

Make a bowl of mayonnaise yourself, or cheat using the method described on p. 19.

Chop into bite-sized pieces:

Cauliflower	Carrots
Celery	Green peppers
Mushrooms	Red peppers
Radishes	Fennel

and anything else you fancy that is in season

Invite guests to dip away and to be as friendly as they like.

Artichokes

Artichokes are ice-breakers. It's amazing how many people are shy to admit that they have no idea how to eat them. (Sluts have no problems when it comes to asking questions: the only problem is when someone tells them to mind their own business.) I once served six people with a mound each of asparagus, another vegetable that presents problems to many. I was delayed in the kitchen for the whole of that course trying to persuade the cat to let go of the second course (a duck) which she had hidden behind the fridge and was defending with her life. When I arrived at the table, everyone was sitting around looking troubled. They had all munched their way carefully through the stalks of the asparagus and had left the heads. Many people encounter even greater difficulty when faced with an artichoke. So do your guests the favour of offering to educate anyone who is a novice. If you yourself are unacquainted with the art of artichoke-eating, speak right up and ask a friend.

Boiling artichokes takes about an hour. As soon as a leaf comes away easily in your hand, they are ready. Serve them hot with melted butter or cold with mayonnaise. Some guests may find it tricky to separate the heart from the hair; it's worth seeing that they do it properly as they can choke horribly if the little hairs get caught in their throat.

Broad Bean and Cucumber Salad

1 lb very young broad beans	Vinaigrette dressing
	2 cloves garlic
½ cucumber	2 eggs (optional)

Pod the beans and dice the cucumber, keeping the skin on. Make a vinaigrette (see pp. 122–4), adding the crushed garlic and, unless you prefer a very sharp taste, a teaspoon of brown sugar. Let the vegetables marinate in this for at least 1 hour before serving. If you want a really rich sauce, softboil 2 eggs for 2½ minutes and then scoop out the yolks and stir them into the dressing.

Tomato Salad

6 large and beautiful
  tomatoes
1 large Spanish onion or
  2 small onions
4 cloves garlic
4 tablespoons olive oil

1 tablespoon vinegar
1 teaspoon brown sugar
½ jar capers
A handful of parsley
Salt and black pepper

Slice the tomatoes as thinly as possible. Chop the onion into tiny cubes. Use live-in lover for this job, or stuff a piece of bread between your lips. If you feel you might get lifted off to the funny farm for doing this, try wearing dark glasses instead. Another tip to prevent you crying is to put the onion under the tap while you cut it, the idea being to block off the juice which evaporates and attacks your eyes. It is said (by my current, American live-in lover) that if you refrigerate the onions overnight they won't sting your eyes.

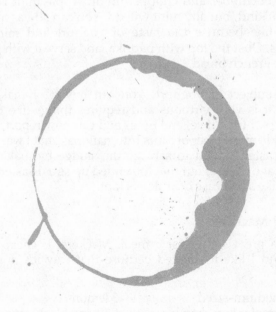

Pour over the olive oil and vinegar, and add the sugar and garlic. Cover with lots of black pepper and salt. Let it marinate for several hours and then refrigerate. Just before serving, add loads of parsley.

Garlic bread goes very well with this salad. You can make it by cutting all the way up a French loaf and spreading butter and garlic in between the slices. Stick it in a hot oven for half an hour and serve with the salad.

Cucumber and Mint Salad

Amazingly-good-for-you salad.

1½ cucumbers	Salt and black pepper
1 pint yoghurt	Masses of apple mint

Chop the cucumber into tiny squares. Put it in a colander with salt to sweat out the juice, and leave for at least 2 hours.

I get fresh Cyprus sheep's yoghurt from Adamou's and add the cucumber and chopped mint. Apple mint is my favourite kind, but any mint will do. You can add as much as you like because the taste of yoghurt and mint is delicious. Dust the top with paprika, and serve it with pitta bread or French bread.

On the subject of yoghurt, you can buy it or make it. Making it is very virtuous and requires things like thermometers. I tried it several times and can now report, as a fully paid-up member of Sluts International, that I was met with disaster. I tried to salvage the sludge by making it into cottage cheese, but that too ended up as a disaster and looked like a bad case of athlete's foot.

Smoked Mackerel

Fish is a great starter for a meal. Mackerel is cheap and tasty, and I like it smoked because that way it's not too oily.

6 medium-sized smoked mackerel	3 lemons
	Salt and black pepper

If you can bear the fish glaring up at you reproachfully, leave the heads on. Otherwise, remove the heads and tails, and split the fish open down the stomach. Lift out the backbone if you wish, or leave the guests to do it themselves. All the dish needs is wedges of lemon and black pepper. I serve it with wholemeal brown bread.

My Sister's Day-before Kippers

My sister is an excellent cook at times: this recipe is one of her good efforts. Make it 24 hours before serving.

6 medium or 8 small	3 cloves garlic
kippers	¼ pint olive oil
6 lemons	Parsley
1 onion	Black pepper

First take the skins off the kippers, then cut them into matchsticks. Squeeze the juice of the lemons over them and add the olive oil, garlic, chopped onion and black pepper. Put the dish on top of the fridge (to keep it away from the cats) and turn the fish over every time you go past for a swig of gin. Twenty-four hours later the lemon juice will have pickled the kippers, and the gin will have had the same effect on you. Either way, both of you will taste delicious.

Everyone loves this dish, which is why I always make more than I need. Keep a supply of it in the fridge, as it can be eaten at any time of the day. It just needs a loaf of bread and a bit of thou.

Snails

Snails are delicious if you are a garlic addict: really, they are just an excuse for loads of garlic butter. Fortunately the snails don't seem to have heads or horns, otherwise I don't think I could eat them.

I did try to cook them from scratch when I was in Spain. I took a bag full of live snails home from the market and stuck them in salt, flour and water as instructed, and jammed on a lid. Four hours later I approached the pot with caution, expecting to find a moribund mound of molluscs. I lifted the lid and was confronted by a seething mass of very angry and very much alive snails. I let them go. Buy them in tins.

6 snails per person	½ lb butter
1 clove of garlic per	Salt and black pepper
person	Parsley

Follow the directions on the tin, and then serve some French bread. Even guests who have never tried snails before will like to use the bread to mop up the juice, which is simply made by melting the butter with the crushed garlic, olive oil, parsley and black pepper.

Posh people have special snail plates and snail holders. Junk shops often have the indented plates from hotels and restaurants, and toothpicks do just as well as the fancy holders. The slut can thus be inexpensively yet thoroughly equipt.

It is possible, by the way, to eat English garden snails. Stick out a warning sign that if they persist in eating your garden, you will retaliate. Just be sure to hide the sign from Aunt Maude, the rabid member of the RSPCA.

For a totally different starter, serve the following. It seemed such an odd idea that I tried it, and was converted.

Baked Potato and Caviar

| 6 small potatoes (ask for | 2 pots lumpfish roe |
| floury ones) | ½ pint sour cream |

Put a nail through each of the potatoes, as they will cook far quicker that way. Bake them in a hot oven for 45 minutes. When you take them out roll them between your hands to make the insides fluffy when opened.

Mix the sour cream with the lumpfish roe and spoon the mixture into the split potatoes. Serve with black pepper. If you can get fresh chives, chop them and add them to the mixture.

Lemon Mushrooms on Toast

Most people like mushrooms, and on a cold winter's evening they make a good first course.

2 lb mushrooms	¼ lb butter
3 lemons	Salt and pepper
1 tablespoon olive oil	

Try to get the flat, black, autumn mushrooms that taste of the farmyard; they absorb the lemon juice so much better. Heat the olive oil and butter together, and then add the lemon juice. Wait until it bubbles and add the mushrooms. Put a lid on the saucepan and shake it every few minutes until the mushrooms are covered in the oil and are about to collapse. Serve them on toast and add salt and pepper to taste.

Marrow Bone Rings

Sluts make friends everywhere because they are insatiably curious. In fact, most sluts know their local shops and shopkeepers intimately, so shopping is a royal progression of news and views. Our local butcher is M. Reilly's, and each piece of meat bought takes several minutes of discussion. (Apart from anything else, we're all Irish.)

If your butcher is your friend he will make sure you get the best cuts of meat, and can help out when you are experimenting with something new. Marrow bones are not new, but most people ignore them unless they have a dog. Sluts always spend a few pence on marrow bones because they make such beautiful soups and take no effort apart from changing the water a few times to get rid of the fat. This recipe is simple as long as you can persuade your butcher to saw some 2-inch rings off a large marrow bone.

6 rings of marrow bone	Salt and pepper
Fresh toast	

Preheat the grill. Put the rings under the grill for 10 minutes each side. Serve with hot toast, salt and pepper. Give everyone a teaspoon to dig the marrow out.

If you worry about presentation, you can get the marrow bones a day in advance and soak them, changing the water three or four times. This will ensure that they look a nice pink colour when you serve them. Without the soaking they taste just as good, but are a rather unappetizing grey colour. If this puts you off, smother the marrow bones with chopped parsley.

Fennel and Cheese

Fennel isn't usually eaten in England. It has a lovely aniseed taste, and can be served as a cooked first course or as a vegetable dish, or used finely chopped in salad. Here is one way to prepare fennel as a starter.

4 medium-sized fennel	2 tablespoons butter
White sauce	Salt and pepper
Parmesan cheese	

Fennel is a white, bulbous vegetable with a few strands of lacy vegetation on the top. Cut off the base and the tops, and remove the tough outer leaves. Slice the fennel into 1-inch slices. Brown them in the butter and then simmer for at least 25 minutes. Pour over the white sauce and add the grated cheese. I always put a bowl of cheese on the table because some people love lots of it.

Making white sauce is yet another trying test for any cook. Organized cooks seem to have little trouble, while sluts often find that the sauce tends to suffer from a recurring 'lump' disease. The best way to make this sauce is to keep packets of ready-mix in the cupboard and just add milk. For the righteous, I give instructions for home-made white sauce. For the rest of us, read what it says on the packet.

Personally, I never make any sauce that I can buy in a packet. All those years of sweating over a saucepan which contained massive unyielding lumps of congealed flour taught me a lesson. Not only was the sense of failure awful, but so were the fevered minutes of trying to strain the stuff through a sieve while guests sat waiting. Finally, the ultimate humiliation of chucking the whole lot through the window on to unsuspecting passers-by drove me into

34

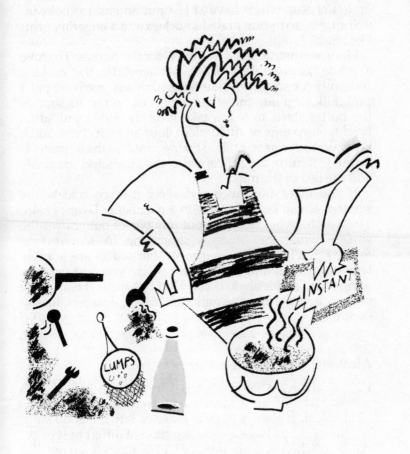

PERSONALLY I NEVER MAKE
ANY SAUCE that I CAN
BUY IN A PACKET

the supermarket to find the forbidden alternatives. Thank God for packet sauces. Thank God also for packets of grated cheese which have at last put an end to cooks involuntarily acquiring grated knuckles and a lingering goat-like smell.

Here are instructions, however, for the purists. To make a white sauce, called Sauce Béchamel by the cooking fraternity (or sorority), take two saucepans. Into one put 1 pint milk, and into the other put 1½ oz butter. As soon as the butter starts to foam, take it off the stove and add 2 level tablespoons of sifted plain flour and stir. Now add a little of the warm milk, stirring until a thick paste is formed. Return the saucepan to the stove and gradually add the rest of the milk.

If you leave the sauce and allow it to go cold before serving, it will be covered with a disgusting layer of skin. The way to avoid this is to put tiny bits of butter over the surface while the sauce is simmering. A seal is thus formed. It all sounds very simple, but sauces are horribly temperamental, and at the point where you add the milk lumps tend suddenly to occur. Don't panic. Just reach for a packet. If you warm the milk, the stuff in a packet doesn't curdle.

Alcoholic Chicken Liver Pâté

Pâté is always a good starter. I hate being served with mingy slabs of grey meat paste decorated with a limp lettuce leaf. It always pays to make or buy the good stuff, and most shops have a wide selection of different types of pâté. So when you are tired or bad-tempered, go out and buy a good wedge and plant it on the table with a pile of thick, warm toast and sliced lemons.

However, if you have the energy – and sluts tend to have bursts of it – try making this pâté.

2 lb chicken liver	¼ bottle brandy
5 cloves garlic	Salt and black pepper to
1 lb butter	taste

Send lover to shop with mixer to get it mended. If shop

IF you are PRONE
to IMBIBE,
do BE CAREFUL

makes rude remarks about state of mixer, borrow long-suffering neighbour's mixer. Promise to keep music below Concorde level for next two weeks to mollify her.

Next, melt butter in a large frying pan. Crush the garlic and fry it until it browns.

Chuck in the chicken livers. If you buy them in a supermarket, the bits of gristle and gunge are usually removed. If you buy them from your local butcher they tend to be warm and bloody, having just been ripped out of a chicken. In this case it is, therefore, wise to remove anything that looks like an artery.

Stir the livers around until they change colour and a brown gravy invades the foaming butter.

Now add the brandy. By this time, I have saved the required quarter of a bottle and have drunk the rest. The reason why cooks set fire to their food is not, as I had always assumed, because they hate their guests, but because the flames consume the alcohol that would give the dish a bitter taste and just leave the full aroma of the wine or brandy. It is extremely embarrassing to find oneself hunched over the kitchen stove naively trying to set light to a recalcitrant dish. The secret is to pour the brandy into a ladle and hold it over the stove until it is warm. Then light it, still in the ladle, and pour it over the dish. If you are prone to imbibe, do be careful. I've followed instructions religiously and still ended up with a funeral pyre between my hands that left no eyebrows, eyelashes or hair as far back as my ears. Mind you, the local hospital thought 'setting light to chicken livers' was a new perversion. They made an appointment with the resident psychiatrist for me, but he turned out to need more help than I did.

When the flames die down (if they don't, call the fire brigade and look to the next section for feeding the five thousand, as firemen have large appetites) pour the whole lot into the mixer. Whiz it round until it is a mush.

Once it looks like the stuff out of baby tins, pour it into an appropriate dish. The butter should rise to the top, but if for some reason it doesn't, heat ¼ lb butter until it runs and pour it over the mixture. This ensures a seal.

Next day you will have a perfect pâté and a dreadful hangover.

Serve the pâté with toast as a starter, or with French bread and a salad for lunch.

Ratatouille

(Otherwise known as 'A Mess of Vegetables')

2 green peppers	5 cloves garlic
2 large onions	A sprig of parsley
(preferably Spanish,	Rosemary
as they are sweet)	2 cups olive oil
4 tomatoes	Salt and black pepper
1 aubergine	Grated Parmesan
3 courgettes	cheese (optional)

Heat the olive oil and then add the crushed garlic. Next chop the vegetables into ¼-inch thick rounds and fry the onions, aubergines and green peppers at a fierce heat until they start to disintegrate (about 10–15 minutes). Add the courgettes and tomatoes and simmer the whole lot until you have had a bath and a stiff gin. Come back into the kitchen, pour another drink, and taste the food. Depending on your tastebuds, add salt, pepper and, if you're feeling cheerful, some black olives. This dish will stew nicely for ages. Serve it with a thick coat of parsley, French bread and a bowl of grated Parmesan cheese.

Soups are a slut's basic religion. Whatever else she can or cannot afford, an ongoing soup is always present on the back of the stove. Not for her is the agony of the Cordon Bleu. Instead, the casserole is used as a receptacle for all the cooking waste of the week and the dregs of the wine. The whole becomes a filling, life-enhancing broth so that no traveller leaves the house unrefreshed. The house always smells of the latest soup.

Onion Soup

6 large Spanish onions	1 pint home-made beef
6 cloves garlic	stock or 2 tins
4 tablespoons olive oil	Campbell's beef
1 tablespoon sugar	consommé

Use a thick casserole and heat the olive oil slowly. Add 4 of the 6 cloves of garlic, chopped, and fry them until they brown.

Add the onions which you have sliced into thin rings. Sprinkle the sugar over the onions and stir until the sugar just begins to catch. This gives an interesting caramelized taste to the soup.

Fry the onions until they brown, and then add the meat stock if you have made it or the tinned consommé that you buy if you are like me.

Simmer the soup for 40 minutes. Chop up the remaining 2 cloves of garlic for the toast. Make 6 slices, butter them, and then lay on a slice of garlic and pile high with Parmesan cheese. Float the cheesy garlic toast in the bowls of soup.

Consommé

I don't know why I like this so much, but the idea of a clear cup of soup topped with fresh lemon juice as a beginning to a meal is unquestionably irresistible.

Making your own consommé is time-consuming, but it is still well within the slut's philosophy of cooking. However, as any slut has an immediate alternative, you can always reach for the tins.

Ask your butcher – with whom, as already instructed, you should have an intimate relationship – to cut a large marrow bone into manageable pieces, and head for home.

The bone has to be soaked for 24 hours, and you should skim off the water every time you walk past as it will look like a malarial swamp. Next day, when you stagger down stairs for a swig of Alka-Seltzer and Nescafé, stuff the bones into a stew pot. Cover them with water and throw in 3 large unpeeled onions. Turn on the stove to a temperature that just shivers the water (e.g. 200° F on an electric stove, gas mark 1), and go back to bed. Six hours later, the marrow will have vacated the bones. Strain the soup. Add salt, pepper and lemon juice to taste. If you want to eat it cold, leave it overnight in the fridge; the next day it will have set. Serve it with slices of lemon and toast.

If you can't be bothered to make it yourself because your lover has left, or your boss is impossible, buy 2 cans of Campbell's consommé, put them in the fridge for at least 4 hours if you want to have the consommé cold, and serve with lemon juice and black pepper.

Trachinas

It looks like a packet of mouse-droppings. I asked Adam of Adamou's to explain one day when I was browsing in the back of the shop. 'Cracked wheat and yoghurt soup,' he said, in between snatches of Kant and Rilke. Naki, his brother, offered an extra recipe: it really is delicious if you like lemons and yoghurt.

Simply add 6 cups of water to 1 cup of trachinas. Simmer this mixture for 20 minutes and you have a very tasty soup. If you want something more filling, add a large tin of tomatoes and slices of haloumi cheese. Serve it with pitta bread and lemon juice.

Chicken Soup

This shouldn't need much explanation. If you have the slut's habit of keeping a large pot on the back of the stove, you will probably have a chicken carcass or bones at least once during the week. The reason why most people shy away from stew pots is that we have all been frightened to death by stories of salmonella poisoning. Furthermore, kitchens are now designed to hide the existence of cooking pots, for the pots are put away behind nasty panelled doors. Actually, if you boil the stew pot every day for at least 20 minutes, no microbes will survive and the taste of the soup will improve.

1 chicken carcass	4 cloves garlic
6 tablespoons olive oil	4 large potatoes
8 carrots	Salt and pepper
3 onions	

Fry the onions in the olive oil along with the garlic until they brown. Chop the carrots into 1-inch pieces and stir. Put the carcass in the pot and add chicken stock or 2 chicken stock cubes with sufficient water to cover the carcass. You can add a cup of white wine or cider at this stage if you like. Let it simmer for as long as possible – all day is best – remembering to add extra water if too much evaporates. An hour before serving, remove the bones and add 4 large potatoes cut into quarters. The starch from the potatoes will thicken the soup, and the mixture of soup and potatoes is delicious.

Have this soup as a filling first course on a cold night, or use a whole chicken and serve it as a main course with many more vegetables such as leeks, green peppers and parsnips. I often make it at the weekend. I serve it on a Saturday night, and then put what is left back on the stove on Sunday, rummaging round the fridge for oddments of veg like cabbage and more onions and potatoes. I add more chicken cubes and then stir in 2 heaped tablespoons of Madras curry powder, so on Sunday night we have curry soup with French bread.

Remember, curry was invented to disguise the taste of rotting meat. Every slut has tins of curry powder to hand. Whatever happens, however disastrous, you can always curry it.

Corn Chowder

This is essentially an American dish. It is easy to put to-gether and can be enlarged to make a main course with a good salad. 'Chowder' comes from an archaic French word *chaudmer*, meaning fish soup.

I use corn, but you can also substitute clams for corn and have a clam chowder.

2 slices bacon	2 medium tins corn
2 small onions	or the equivalent
7 cups milk	frozen corn
¾ lb potatoes	

Cut the bacon into small pieces and fry it until it runs. Add the onions and stir-fry for 12 minutes. When the onion rings start to go brown, add the milk and then the potatoes. Do something else for 10 minutes and then come back to test the potatoes. If they have cooked, add the corn and leave it all to simmer for 15 minutes. Do see that the milk doesn't boil over.

If you decide to make this a main dish, just increase all the quantities.

Gazpacho

Everyone who loves cooking has his or her own version of Gazpacho. It's easy to make if you have a blender, otherwise it takes ages to chop everything. So it is definitely worth making if you can coerce someone to do the chopping for you. This recipe is enough for six people, with some left over for the next day. Sluts always cook for an army. If you are going to cook for six people, you might as well cook enough to have leftovers for the next day, which means you either eat the same thing twice because you like it so much or you add various other spices and sauces to turn it into something else. Gazpacho is definitely something most people will eat until it comes out of their ears.

3 large ripe tomatoes	4 cloves garlic
1 large onion	1 cup olive oil
1 red pepper	Parsley
1 cucumber	Tarragon (optional)
1 large tin Italian tomatoes	Salt and black pepper

Chop the fresh vegetables in small squares or use a blender and put them all into a large bowl in which you have already crushed the garlic. Take care not to lose the juice. If you're using a blender you will have little problem, but if you're chopping, the juice tends to run down the draining board and into your shoes.

Add the tin of tomatoes and cut them into the soup. Add lots of fresh black pepper, salt and chopped parsley. By now it looks delicious. Pour the olive oil over it all and stir it in. Within a few minutes, the oil will rise to the top and seal the aroma into the soup. Put the soup in the fridge to cool until you are ready to serve it.

Tzacik (or Bulgarian Cucumber Soup)

This is another good summer soup.

6 cups plain yoghurt	2 cloves garlic
1½ cups buttermilk	1 tablespoon white wine
2 medium cucumbers	vinegar
3 tablespoons finely	1 tablespoon olive oil
chopped dill	Salt and pepper to taste
1 tablespoon finely	
chopped mint	

Mix the yoghurt and the buttermilk together for a few minutes. Cut the cucumber up into very small squares. Add them to the mixture with the spices, garlic, salt and pepper. Add the vinegar drop by drop. Then add the oil the same way. Stick it all in the fridge. If it's a very hot day, put an ice-cube into the soup bowls when serving.

If you are pushed for time, the following two recipes are very quick.

Grilled Grapefruit

3 large grapefruit   6 tablespoons sugar

Cut the grapefruit in half and spread a heaped tablespoon of sugar over each section. Stick the halves under the grill if you have enough room, or into a very hot oven until the sugar turns brown and starts to bubble. Serve it hot or leave it to go cold.

Greek Salad

2 green peppers	2 cloves garlic
2 large tomatoes	Olive oil
1 large onion	¼ lb feta cheese

Slice the green peppers and tomatoes and put them in a dish. Crush the garlic and add it in with the olive oil. Put the onion rings on the top and then add slices of feta cheese. Serve it with pitta bread.

Most of these first courses require very little organizing once you get the ingredients together. When a slut gives a meal, it's more of a spontaneous event than a planned action. Wandering past your local shops, you can soon see what's in season. After you discover your own cooking style, throwing things together becomes second nature. You will come to trust your own creative instincts and abilities instead of always believing that there is some dark magic learned by other people that enables them to produce perfect food. Good soups and salads are a complete meal unto themselves – far more enjoyable than course after course of indifferent and tasteless food that merely looks pretty. Confidence comes with practice. So does the assurance to be your own sloppy self and not struggle to keep up with the lady next door who is giving herself a nervous breakdown trying to impress her husband's friends.

First courses are designed to give people time to relax after arriving at the house and get to know each other. That's why they should be easy to prepare and no sweat to serve. There are few things worse than an apprehensive hostess urging guests to the table when what they want is to sip their drinks at their own leisure and eye each other up and down. Sluts let people sit where they like. (One thing worse is sitting the local letch at the other end of the table from the local lay. If you sit them next to each other, they can grope happily between courses.) Smokers naturally tend to congregate. If separated, they cough and hack over the non-smokers' food. Anyway it's interesting to see just who decides to sit next to whom. The nicest part of six people getting together for an evening is the phone calls the next morning. It's amazing what people get up to one night, only to be attacked by convenient amnesia the morning after. The booze will have helped.

Booze is always tricky for gatherings. If you have lots of money you can simply have a huge range of spirits and aperitifs on display and let people help themselves. After all, most people like their drinks according to their own tastes, and it's infuriating to have to suffer someone else's version of your gin and tonic. Also, if the hostess is rushing round fixing drinks, she no sooner gets to number six than number one wants another. So she ends up with scorch marks on the carpet as she zooms about like a demented bluebottle. It is far better to have self-help dinner parties, even if Harry is well known for by-passing the glasses and swigging straight from the bottle. If he's going to get plastered, he'll do it anyway. Besides, it's much easier to pile him into a corner than to have him crash face-first into the main course.

If you are impoverished, and most sluts are because they spend all they get on having a good time, then it's cheap plonk for most occasions. Try to avoid the thin stuff that rots the gut and turns the teeth brown. This is usually Spanish or comes from somewhere like Indo-China. French wine is usually drinkable and much of it is cheap. With sluts' cooking, which is very much peasant-style, a really expensive wine would be lost in all the garlic and spices. Anyway, most sluts and their friends put away so much wine during a meal that no one could be rich enough to supply anything other than cheap plonk.

It is worth decanting a red wine several hours before serving it because the air or whatever (it can get very technical) makes the wine taste less acid and more mellow. If you discover that the white wine is horrible, just get it so cold that you can barely taste it and then keep popping ice-cubes into people's glasses. It is a good idea to find a reliable cheap wine locally and stick to it. Ideally, you should train your guests to bring bottles of good wine which you then shove into a back cupboard and serve your own. The good wine can be shared at a later date between you and your beloved alone.

TWO
FISH, FLESH AND FOWL

spike their bottles

FISH, FLESH AND FOWL

Sluts have the good sense to serve easy main courses that virtually cook themselves. If you wish to put any effort into a main course, then cut out the first course. Whatever you do, don't work hard. People are to be enjoyed, and so is food. All these recipes for main courses are based on large helpings, because sluts do not believe in lots of little side dishes that only clutter up the table. The idea is that the main dish *is* the main course, except in a few instances, and a salad follows.

It is a good idea to have a rummage round the local second-hand shops where you can find different-coloured plates and bowls. Then if your guests get drunk or one of the couples decides to resolve a grievance by flinging stuff at each other, it doesn't matter. The same applies to wine glasses. Sluts lose everything, and if they don't lose it they break it. Cheap wine glasses are no loss when lost or broken. I get mine from Kitchenobelia or Habitat for under a pound. I also collect second-hand pâté bowls from a local delicatessen. The lovely brown ones are only 75p. You can use them for salads or soups.

Cut down as far as possible on masses of different plates and knives and forks. They only create lots of washing-up and are more things to be lost or broken. There are plenty of hostesses who spend their lives surrounded by prestigious sets of china and glass. Good for them. A really elegant meal can be a pleasure in someone else's home. The truth of the matter is that sluts cannot give elegant meals because they have crowds of children and animals, all of whom have nasty habits of invading the table. If a slut has not yet reached the children stage, she might well be trying to keep up with 'Superwoman', but she very rarely succeeds.

It is worth getting salt and pepper shakers that actually allow the stuff to run out, rather than risking giving yourself a hernia with the peppermill. The other snag is the salt pot that pours the salt so freely over the food that polite guests end up with their tongues stuck to the roof of their mouths and less polite ones spit their food all over the table.

Candles are always a good idea. I once forgot to pluck a chicken for dinner, and, about two hours before everyone arrived, remembered that I'd put it in the deep freeze. I took it out frozen solid and stuck it in a pan of hot water. After about half an hour, it was possible to wrench the feathers off the deceased bird. An hour later, it looked like an outraged porcupine. Sluts never panic – they get drunk. I curried the chicken and the guests arrived. Two very pretty candles illuminated the table and the chicken lurked in a sea of curry sauce. No one could see what they were eating, so they all enjoyed it. I didn't eat it. In case of botulism, someone had to refrain in order to summon the ambulance and notify the next-of-kin. The moral of this story is: when in doubt, curry it and light the candles. (If it smells, use scented candles.)

Dressing for dinner is no problem for sluts because they don't bother. These days, there are comfortable night-dresses sold by shops like Night Owls which are pure cotton with pretty smocked tops. French Connection make loose shirts in lovely colours, and sluts buy from both these shops. You can live in these clothes. Rise in the morning, put on a top, and you are dressed for the day. There is nothing more boring than spending time worrying about clothes or shopping for them. Sluts give each other garments discovered at jumble sales or unearthed from Aunt Agatha's shed. In fact, sluts always look co-ordinated in a chaotic sort of way. If the weather gets colder, they just add more layers.

No self-respecting slut owns an iron. Anything you put on will in time lose its creases. Clothes get used to not being ironed and soon cease to expect it. Sluts very rarely

when it doubt, CURRY it + LiGHt the caNDLes

wear shoes except for simple sandals in the summer and warm boots in the winter. It's other people who seem to have problems with the slut's sense of dress. Nowadays, if it's going to be a formal night out, any slut worth her salt can find something loose and Indian. Sluts don't expect their guests to dress up, and men are never expected to wear ties or jackets. The rule is to make yourself and other people comfortable.

If you are going to start with the main course, it's a good idea to put some small eats out with the drinks. This gives you time to sort out the last minute bits and pieces, and allows the guests time to settle in for a good evening of sex and scandal. Indian shops have lots of good spicy biscuits and nuts. Japanese seaweed crackers are interesting. Don't get into the time-consuming business of making stuff for this part of the evening. The guests are far too busy chatting each other up and swigging back the booze to care about how much effort you make. They just want to get their teeth and hands round something tasty, so keep it all simple and invite your favourite slag.

Lucy is my dinner party success. I hate having her to stay because sluts and slags have very different lifestyles. Sluts throw everything into cupboards and forget it all; slags throw everything on the floor and leave it all. Lucy's room takes twenty-four hours to silt up and two weeks to muck out. Lucy removes her inch-thick mascara with a huge jar of cold cream, which is fine except that she also stubs her fags out in it. It is not a pretty sight. Neither is Lucy first thing in the morning. She diets furiously so she has an excellent figure. However, she had to make a decision about alcohol. Giving it up meant she would eat more, so she decided to give up eating and stick to drinking, which is all right for her but hard on everybody else.

She is, nonetheless, lively and much in demand. Of course, I do have trouble with other people's wives who hold me responsible for their husbands' desertions. Lucy has a good heart and never keeps the husbands very long. If she is staying the night in my house, I make her give them back before the end of the evening, because I hate seeing them staggering about my kitchen the next morning sodden with alcohol and guilt.

51

If a slut has children, these too must be dealt with before the main course. Sluts' children are very good about dinner parties. They extract large sums of money to go to the pictures or to remain out of the way. When the children are little, sluts spike their bottles or fill their little mitts with bars of chocolate. If they are old enough to join in, they are threatened with death if they repeat their mother's opinions about the assembled company. Sluts' children either follow in their mothers' footsteps or become complete opposites and die of embarrassment at the mere sight of their mothers. Sluts have an easy-going attitude towards children which is parallel to their attitude towards animals and men: all they need is a lot of good food, lots of love, and not too much close attention, and they will thrive.

Sluts love growing things but are incapable of looking after plants regularly, so they house only those plants that believe in self-help and that virtually look after themselves. Plants disguise peeling wallpaper as well as stains on the carpets. Unfortunately, as sluts can't train anything, let alone themselves, the plants tend to grow rampant and threaten to overpower the guests. Do not believe stories of drunken guests claiming that their drinks were snatched out of their hands by a thirsty Umbrella plant.

Herbs feature largely in the slut's repertoire. Every year, she repairs to her nearest nursery to buy an instant garden. A neat row of parsley, thyme, sage and marjoram on the window-sill makes her feel smugly virtuous. Larger pots of geraniums in the garden look positively Mediterranean, and no weeding is necessary. I go to Crabtree Gardens on Crabtree Lane where a long-suffering woman listens to my tales of woe, and then selects for me plants with iron constitutions. She also has rare fresh herbs like French tarragon, which is much stronger than other sorts of tarragon.

After a busy ten minutes of overseeing my estate, which consists of six pots of geraniums and a dozen assorted herb-baskets, I retire to the kitchen with several sweet-scented sprigs, feeling healthy and fulfilled. 'The country life,' I sigh, and settle down with a stiff drink to watch 'Gardener's World'.

Lucy put her plants on the pill, figuring that the hormones would do them good. They went berserk, and throbbed with unslaked lust. Finally, she woke up one day to find them all crashed out on the floor. The local family planning clinic was not helpful.

There is nothing worse than a plant that sits there suffering with a terminal illness. Sluts give ailing plants away to organized friends who revive them. Sluts' gardens are usually original and weed-infested. However, when the weather is good, sluts like to entertain outside. After a large jug of Pimms (½ bottle of gin, ½ bottle of Pimms No. 1, mixed with enough fizzy lemonade to fill the jug to the brim; add chopped apple, oranges, lemons and cucumber, and sprigs of fresh apple mint) the garden looks delightful. Even the smell of tom-cat begins magically to fade away. Always remember that style without effort is the hallmark of the true slut.

FISH

Do make friends at your local wet-fish shop. Fresh fish is so much more tasty than the frozen sort. You should choose a fish that lies there looking furious, as if it is about to leap out at you. If it's dull and flaccid, that's how it will taste. Lots of people don't buy fish because they feel apprehensive about the heads and tails. Actually, fish are easy to gut and clean. It's a pity to let the fishmonger remove the heads because so much of the taste of the dish will come from the bits that are usually thrown away. In China the cheek of the fish, found just below the eyes, is considered the best bit. Just like the 'oyster' of a chicken which is found in two shallow indentations on the chicken's back, the rather unappetizing parts of a fish often have the most taste. Certainly, scaling a fish is a boring job and is best left to those at the shop, who will also gut and clean the fish if you so request. I have a cat

iF he tHREATENS to FAINT, PROP hiM uP
against tHE DRAINING
BOARd with a dRINK +
tELL hiM to
get oN with it

who loves guts, so I take the whole fish home. I then slit it up the middle, remove the guts, and wash it out. Sluts have to remember that not everyone shares their earthy approach to life. Some people, oddly enough, are very put off by a whole fish glaring at them accusingly from a plate. Most sluts reckon it's worth cooking the whole fish anyway, and bank on the fact that starvation will drive everyone to the table.

Prawn and Scallop Vol-au-Vents

6 large vol-au-vent cases	6 spring onions
6 large or 12 small scallops	3 tablespoons sherry
1½ lb peeled prawns	1½ pints white sauce
½ lb butter	A large bunch of parsley
¼ lb mushrooms	1½ lb rice

You can buy perfectly good vol-au-vent cases, either fresh or frozen, in most supermarkets, bakeries and delicatessens. Only masochists or nuns make them. It's always worth keeping a stock of them in the cupboard because you can make this sort of dish with leftovers. It always tastes good and is very filling. The prawns should be fresh if possible: they are sold ready-peeled in wet-fish shops. Do try to avoid frozen prawns as they usually taste like ancient blotting paper. Marks and Spencer's sell the best frozen prawns. (In fact, I get most of my frozen food from there. Although it is more expensive I know it will taste good, especially the chicken.) The scallops too should be fresh. If you must buy frozen, make sure you buy a good brand. If you get them fresh, cleaning them is just a matter of scooping them off the shell and taking out the black vein that runs around the perimeter of the scallop. Wash them under running water because they are quite sandy.

Sit the vol-au-vent cases in a large flat oven-proof dish.

In a saucepan, melt 2 oz butter. When it foams, chop in the spring onions, including the green tails. Add the sliced mushrooms and stir until they are softened. Put in the prawns and the scallops. Let them heat through.

55

Add 3 tablespoons of sherry and remove the mixture from the heat. Now make 1½ pints of white sauce. You can do this the virtuous way (see p. 36), or use a packet and a half of ready-made sauce. Either way, once you have made the sauce, mix it into the prawn and scallop mixture. Turn the sauce into the vol-au-vent cases and pour the remaining liquid round the bases.

Put the dish into a preheated oven of 325° F, gas mark 2. Let it all heat thoroughly for 30 minutes. If you want to make the dish ahead of time, go as far as cooking the fish and sauce separately. Put the whole thing together as the guests arrive and let it warm through. If you let it hang about for much more than half an hour, the vol-au-vent cases tend to go soggy.

Serve it on a bed of rice with lemon wedges.

If you cook this dish too often and find yourself getting bored with it, vary it by using a cheese and tomato sauce. Or try adding a little curry powder to the fish mixture. Good cooking is a matter of learning to trust yourself and having plenty of practice.

You will probably have your own method of cooking rice successfully, but as far as I know the only one that always works is a little rice-boiling contraption you can get in Chinese emporiums or in some large shops. This device is electric and cooks the rice at exactly the right temperature: it never produces gluey, gelatinous rice. However, I use a Malay method taught to me by an amah who got tired of watching me throw the stuff all round the room in a rage. This method seems to work for all types of rice, except brown rice which takes more cooking and therefore requires more water. I use Sea Island Rice which is very full-flavoured, whereas the Uncle Ben's variety is tasteless.

For six people use 1½ lb rice. Put the rice into a thick-bottomed pan. Cover it with an equal amount by volume of cold water. (The amah measured the quantities by sticking her index finger into the rice and then adding an equal height on her finger of water from the tap.) Add about 2 teaspoons of salt. Next bring to the boil and leave it boiling furiously until all the water is gone and holes start to appear in the surface of the rice (about 30 minutes). Take it off the heat, cover it and leave it for a further 10 minutes. It should be fluffy and dry. If not, don't panic. If for some reason you haven't measured it right, and it's still hard to chew after 20 minutes, add more water (enough just to cover the rice), and boil it furiously. If you've added too much water and it's all soggy, put it in a colander and run boiling water through it. Then return it to the pan and let it sit for 10 minutes. If the whole thing is a total disaster, get out two packets of Smash instant potato and pretend you always intended to serve the dish with mashed potatoes.

If cooking rice really makes you nervous, cook it the day before, and then just steam it in a steamer or a colander in a saucepan of boiling water immediately before serving. This way, you can forget about the worry of getting it right on the day. There is nothing worse than having to slap a soggy mass on to people's plates.

Mussel Soup

Moules marinière is an easy and cheap recipe. People who say they don't like mussels really mean that the little things look so vaginal that they find them disgusting. It says a lot about the people who don't like mussels, because it is a delicious dish, and mussels are naturally suited to absorbing wine and herbs.

Most recipes give long instructions about cleaning mussels, so much so that the whole procedure looks so complicated and boring that many people don't attempt it. If you are on holiday by the sea in England, you can usually pick your own. Whether you do this or get them from a fish shop instead, put them in a bucket of water with a large handful of flour and let them settle for the night. The mussels have the equivalent of the hangman's last meal and obligingly purify themselves by cleaning themselves out with the flour. When you are ready to make the soup lift the mussels out of the water, and you will find that all the sand and grit will be left behind at the bottom of the bucket. If there are any mussels floating at the top of the water, throw them out. These are not heroic mussels bent on escape, but are dead creatures.

¾ pint dry white wine
or dry cider
A 6-quart enamelled pan
with cover
6 quarts mussels
8 tablespoons chopped
shallots or finely
chopped onions

A large bunch of parsley
2 bay leaves
½ teaspoon thyme
½ teaspoon black
pepper
3 oz butter

Fry the shallots (or onions) in the butter. When they are soft, add the herbs, stir, then add the wine. Boil for 2–3 minutes. Add 6 quarts of mussels to the pan and put the cover on. Shake the saucepan frequently for a further 5 minutes. The mussels should be cooked and open by this time. Add the chopped parsley and ladle the soup into big bowls. Serve with garlic French bread.

Mussel soup is rich and nourishing. Don't spend hours scrubbing, trying to remove the 'beards'. The beard consists of a few strands of hair that acts as a strainer for the mussel. You are always warned that if you eat it by accident you will suffer a fate worse than death. But if you warn the guests and show them how to pull it out, you will save yourself a lot of time and give them something to do other than just stuffing their faces. If you want to experiment with this soup, try adding 5 oz breadcrumbs to the sauce when cooking it. This makes it much thicker and richer. Or, for a different flavour, add a large tin of Italian plum tomatoes to the sauce.

Squid in Red Wine

Squid looks awful to most people. Really, it's only the tentacles that look so disgusting, along with the little beak in the middle (commonly assumed to be the mouth, this beak is actually the anus). For this stew it's much easier to cook the main part of the body and give the tentacles to the cats who, being English cats, probably won't thank you. You can get fresh squid from fish shops or you can buy frozen squid. Frozen squid are all right for this recipe as it is based on long stewing in a rich sauce. If you do happen to buy the squid fresh, you will find it a messy business removing the ink sac along with the film of slippery skin that encases the squid. The trick is to do it in a bowl of warm water. Actually, the more often you try, the easier it becomes. Having got the hang of it you'll quite enjoy the operation, particularly if you have always harboured delusions of being a famous surgeon or if you grew up with a crush on Dr Kildare.

2 lb squid	½ bottle red wine
4 large onions	1 tablespoon marjoram
2 lemons	1 tablespoon thyme
6 cloves garlic	Salt and black pepper
5 large tomatoes	to taste
3 tablespoons tomato paste	Olive oil

Preheat the oven to 325° F, gas mark 2.

Cut the squid into rings about ¼-inch thick. Cover the bottom of a casserole with olive oil, and fry the chopped onions and crushed garlic until the onions are golden. Then add the tomatoes and the squid. Turn the mixture over until the squid has gone white. Now add the lemon juice. Mix in the tomato paste and the wine, and add the marjoram, thyme, salt and black pepper.

Cook this dish for 1½ hours. Serve with rice. I sometimes add a carton of yoghurt just before serving if I think it's too thin. You can add yoghurt to almost any dish if you are worried about its thinness, and, provided you don't add it while the stew is boiling, you can often salvage the meal.

It is worth knowing that yoghurt is an excellent remedy for burns. If you get the yoghurt on to the burn immediately, it will rarely blister. Sluts do have a bad habit of pouring hot things over themselves and other people, so remember to keep some yoghurt in the fridge.

Salt Codfish and Ackee

This is a traditional West Indian dish, and is usually served with Johnny Cakes, which are like dumplings. The cakes are used to mop up the juice. There is no way that sluts can get dumplings together: they tend to be like bullets if you get them wrong, or else they disintegrate and ruin the meal. I stick to rice.

Ackee – a fruit that grows in the West Indies – is sold in tins in England and looks like scrambled eggs.

2 lb salt codfish	3 tablespoons dried
4 large onions	thyme or basil
4 cloves garlic	2 medium tins ackee
6 tomatoes	Black pepper to taste
4 tablespoons tomato	
paste	

Salt codfish is available in most large shops in immigrant areas. It smells horrible when you buy it, so you must soak it for at least 24 hours, changing the water four or five times.

In a large frying pan, fry the chopped onions and crushed garlic in olive oil until they are golden brown. Add the chopped tomatoes and herbs. Flake the fish with a fork and add it to the sauce. Mix it thoroughly and let it stew for 20 minutes. Now add the drained ackee to the mixture, folding it in. Serve it at once on a bed of rice.

With many dishes, you can make the major part hours – or the day – before. Here, the ackee would not stay firm for long. What you can do therefore is stop once the salt codfish is integrated, and then reheat it and add the ackee just before serving.

Leaving a dish to go cold overnight is another way of marinating, and improves the flavour. Try to do most things well in advance so you can enjoy the evening and have plenty of time to paint your toenails or just soak in the bath.

Fish Fillets in White Wine

You can make this dish with brill, John Dory or turbot. I usually use sole fillets.

12 fillets of sole	1 oz butter
8 shallots	1 bottle white wine
1½ lb mushrooms	

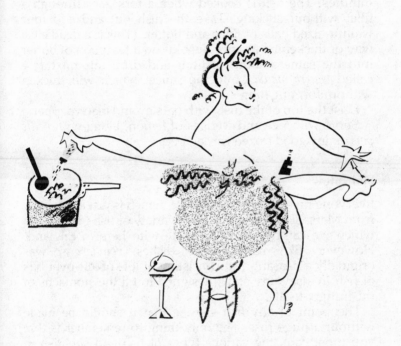

TRY to do MOST things
WELL IN advance so
YOU can enjoy the
EVENING + Have pLENTY
oF time to PaiNt
        YOUR TOE NaiLS

Preheat oven to 350° F, gas mark 4.

Cook the fish in an oven-proof dish. Start on top of the stove, frying the onions in the butter. When the onions are brown, add the thinly sliced mushrooms, and then lay the fish in layers on top. Pour over the wine so that it just covers the fish. Cook in the preheated oven for 15 minutes. The fish is cooked when a fork goes through a fillet without sticking. Take the dish out and add four walnut-sized balls of flour and butter. (This is a dead easy way of thickening a sauce. Just knead a teaspoon of butter into the same amount of flour and drop this mixture – called *beurre manié* – into the sauce, which will thicken without forming lumps.)

Dust the top of the dish with parsley and black pepper.

Serve with rice and wedges of lemon, along with *petits pois* or any good frozen garden peas.

Fish Stew

Everyone raves about *bouillabaisse*, which is just a fish stew from Marseilles. There is a great variety of fish in that area which we can't hope to compete with here in England. However, like many French dishes, *bouillabaisse* was originally a peasant dish consisting of lots of left-over bits of fish in a savoury stew, designed to fill the stomachs of the hungry locals.

The point of any fish stew is that it should be made without a huge fuss. The only thing to remember is that you must cook the various types of fish and shellfish in sequence so that the more delicate morsels do not disintegrate. It is worth looking round for saffron, as this spice adds a lovely colour and taste – and in the case of this particular stew, it will also serve to hoodwink the more squeamish of your guests so that you can add mussels, small octopuses and squid without them knowing.

This recipe is for my version of Hammersmith Fish Stew, otherwise known as Bouillabaisse à la Britain. It is a beautiful stew, and reminds me of hot nights in small Greek villages. It should be served with French bread and salad.

Some or all of the following fish may be used: cod, plaice, sole, John Dory, halibut, haddock, eel, mullet, sea bass, trout, turbot, scallops, mussels, crab, lobster, prawns, octopus and squid. It's a good idea to use some oily fish such as halibut and eel, which will make the sauce thicker. You can make extremely tasty fish soup even with frozen fish because the essential flavour is of tomatoes, onions and leeks, garlic, thyme, olive oil and saffron. Don't panic at the list of ingredients; it's much easier than it looks.

2-inch slices of six or more types of fish (see above)	3½ pints water
	Parsley, bay leaf, thyme
¼ lb chopped onion	2 pinches saffron
¼ lb chopped leeks	1 tablespoon each of
¼ pint olive oil	salt and black pepper
4 crushed cloves garlic	1 pint mussels
1 lb ripe tomatoes	½ lb prawns
3 tablespoons tomato paste	

Ask your fishmonger to chop off pieces of almost any fish he has on the slab that is already cut. This way, you don't have to buy more fish than you actually want. I usually allow about four large chunks of fish per person, plus prawns and mussels.

I don't ever attempt to carry home fish heads and tails and make a fish stock. Quite honestly, it's a good idea only for those who truly love to do it the hard way. These people do, incidentally, end up stinking of fish. Horrible smelly fish bones are left everywhere, and nobody is happy except the cat.

Instead, I buy a pound of cheap fish and put it in with the basic soup while it simmers for 40 minutes. The fish disintegrates, and you don't have to go through the tedium of straining the soup into another saucepan. This method provides the basic fishy taste you need, and you can forget the stock and get on with the soup.

First cook the onions and leeks slowly in the olive oil for 5 minutes or until they become transparent. Stir in the garlic, tomatoes and tomato paste, and cook for a further 5

DO WARN GUESTS THAT THERE ARE SQUIDS IN THE STEW

minutes. Add the water and the herbs and a pound of lean, filleted fish. Simmer the stew for 40 minutes and then taste it. You may need more saffron or thyme.

At this point, cut into large pieces all the fish you need for the final cooking of the soup, separating it on to two plates, one for the tougher fish such as cod, squid, octopus, haddock and eel, the other for the delicate fish like sole and shellfish. Allow two slices of fresh bread for each bowl of soup. Also, put a large bowl of chopped parsley and grated cheese on the table. If you feel faint from all the effort, put the fish in the fridge and pour yourself a large gin. Put your feet up.

You only need 30 minutes to cook the soup just before the guests arrive. If it has been a good day at the fishmonger's, you may have come home with some delightful baby squid or octopus that will make the whole dish taste more authentic. (Do warn guests if they have not been blindfolded that there are squids in the stew, or else they may take fright and assume that there is a monster lurking in the bottom of the soup waiting to wrap its evil legs around their necks and haul them in and drown them.)

After you have settled the guests in with a drink, bring the soup to the simmer for 20 minutes. Add the tougher fish and simmer for 5 minutes. Now put in the cleaned mussels and the delicate fish, and simmer for 5 more minutes. Put the saucepan in the centre of the table and let the guests fill their own soup bowls. Hand round the parsley and the cheese.

Once you get the hang of this dish you can vary it endlessly, making it rich and thick enough to be the only course for dinner. In fact with a soup like this you really only need cheese and salad.

Trout

Trout are so delicious that I serve them as often as I can. Sluts tend to keep things very simple, and fish especially is much nicer when cooked simply. Flash cooks have a horrible habit of putting potatoes and vegetables on the same plate as the fish. It is a revolting practice, because everything then tastes fishy, and you lose the flavour of

SOMe PeOPLe aRe VeRY PUt OFF
BY a WhoLe FiSh GLaRiNG at theM
accuSiNGLY fRoM a PLate

the individual vegetables. If you are going to serve vegetables, put them on a side plate. But quite honestly, fish tastes best as a course on its own. Buy fresh trout. If they are really fresh their bodies will have an iridescent sheen and their eyes will be bright. If there is no fresh trout around, Marks and Spencer sell excellent frozen rainbow trout. These are small, so you will need two for each person.

6 trout (or 12 if small)	Thyme or rosemary
6 shallots	1 oz flour
2 oz butter	Lemons
Salt and black pepper	Brown bread

Preheat oven to 350° F, gas mark 4.

If the fish are fresh, have them gutted by either the fishmonger or your resident lover. I have always found men to be remarkably squeamish when it comes to sticking knives into things and cleaning them out: the mere sight of blood and entrails seems to reduce the average male to a quivering mass. If he threatens to faint, prop him up against the draining board with a drink and tell him to get on with it. Do see that he removes the little sac of slime from the stomach. I didn't bother on one occasion and cooked twenty-four trout which tasted like the contents of the local sewer. There was no rescuing that meal, and that particular lover is still running.

Dry the fish very carefully, because if you cook it wet the skin won't crisp. Soggy fish-skin is extremely unpleasant and reminds me of those disgusting lumps of unidentified sea-creature that they used to serve at school.

It is also worth cutting the fish open when you put them on the plates. People vary in their ability to remove bones. Like lovers, you won't know until they've tried. It is amazing the mess some people can make of a simple fish: by the time they've tried to peel it like a grape and grappled with the backbone, hurling fish all over the table, everyone else is put off.

Trout are marvellously easy to bone because once you've laid them open, you can just lift up the backbone and it will come out clean.

When you have dried the fish, roll them in a dusting of flour which has in it salt, black pepper and thyme or rosemary.

Use a shallow oven-proof dish. On top of the stove, fry the chopped shallots in butter. When the butter foams put the fish in, turning them once so that they are covered in the mixture. Put the dish in the oven for 20 minutes, and do something else like shriek at the children.

Every oven has a mind of its own. One woman's mark 4 is another woman's minus 3 degrees (you can tell a woman's emotional life by her usual oven setting). Sluts' ovens tend to cook everything on full heat, regardless of settings. So don't take recipes too literally. Get to know your oven. After 20 minutes take a look and, armed with a fork, prod the fish. If the fork goes in and comes out without fish sticking to it, you were either too stoned and forgot to put the oven on, in which case you should consult the cat, or else your fish is cooked. Serve it with large wedges of lemon and brown bread and butter.

Salmon with Raisins

I was once given a fish kettle. This is a much treasured kitchen item, largely because it is so big it would take an average-sized shark. It can also be used for the plants or as a cat-tray. However, on the few occasions that I can afford to buy a salmon, the fish kettle is ceremoniously scrubbed out and returned to the stove. If you don't have a fish kettle, you can always use a large casserole and cheese cloth. (A thin nappy will do just as well.) Tie the ends of the cheese cloth to the handles of the casserole so that the fish will be suspended in the steam.

Setting out to buy a whole salmon is a great event. For six people you need a fish weighing 7–8 pounds. Again, your friendly fishmonger will see that it's fresh. Most people will throw up their hands in horror and moan about the expense. These are the very people who give food a bad name by having assorted badly organized courses instead of spending their money on one really delicious course, followed by cheese and fruit.

Salmon is rich and filling. It has delightful pink, moist

flesh that slides down well with chilled white wine. The only nervous moment is deciding whether it is cooked or not. As it is removed from the fish kettle when you go to make the sauce, you have time, if you don't think it's quite cooked, to stick it in a hot oven to finish it off. Fish is much easier than meat when it comes to excavating in order to see if it is cooked through. If you are really unsure, ignore all advice from the books and take a knife and cut down to the bone and have a look. The experts are quite right when they say that by mutilating the fish you will lose some of the juice. But they don't have to sit at the table and watch guests struggle manfully with underdone lumps of fish. If you do have to cut it, make sure you see pinky-white firm flesh all the way down to the bone. If there is a sudden tide-mark of grey flesh, it's not cooked. Put it back.

If it's overcooked and falling off the bone, do a mortuary job. Get a large piece of tinfoil and lay the fish on it. Arrange the fish as best you can, and wrap the foil firmly round it. Put it aside for at least 20 minutes to let it cool down. Give the guests more to drink and then open the parcel gently in the privacy of the kitchen. Don't attempt to remove the foil. Serve it on a plate with the foil tucked snugly around it. It is not such a great disaster if it's over-cooked, for a sauce like the following one makes it moist again.

As I've said before, the one thing you need for cooking anything is confidence, along with the ability to rescue disasters. Sluts take risks all the time because they are not bothered by what other people think of them. However, they do have a sound knowledge of how to make things taste good. Whereas slags usually chuck everything in and get it all wrong, sluts will have tasted a dish all the way through the cooking. Salmon has such a powerful taste of its own, you don't have to worry too much about the flavour.

1 fresh salmon, 7–8 lb	*For the sauce*
4 oz butter	4 egg yolks
2 onions	½ pint thick cream
4 stalks celery	2 heaped tablespoons
2 carrots	raisins

2 bay leaves
A few sprigs of parsley
1 pint dry white wine
Salt and pepper

1 lemon
3 walnut-sized balls
beurre marñie (see
p. 62)
3 tablespoons chopped
parsley

Chuck the butter, onions (sliced), celery (sliced), carrots (sliced), salt, pepper, parsley and bay leaves into the fish kettle and stir over a medium heat with a wooden spoon for about 5–6 minutes.

Add the wine and a pint of water, and boil it all up together. Rub salt over the salmon, both inside and out. (I am assuming you have had the good sense to clean it out and dry it.)

Lay the salmon on a trivet and lower it into the fish kettle, or wrap it in cheese cloth and suspend it over a saucepan.

Cover it tightly and simmer gently for 35–40 minutes. After 40 minutes, remove the fish from the kettle or pan, and have a look at it. If all is well and it looks firm and moist, cover it with foil and put it under a low grill or in the oven warmer while you prepare the sauce.

Strain all the vegetables from the fish kettle and keep the juice. Put this back into the kettle and boil it fast until you have about 1 pint of liquid left. Beat the egg yolks for about 6 minutes. They should be frothy.

Add the cream and continue to beat for a further 5 minutes. Now add a few spoonfuls of the hot broth to the eggs and the cream. This last step makes the egg mixture warm enough to add to the hot broth.

(This is one of the most important lessons you can learn in cooking. If you just slosh the cold cream and eggs into the hot sauce, you end up with a hideous curdled mess. The same thing will happen to any sauce with eggs and cream in it that is allowed to boil. This is why sluts rarely make sauces. You do need to be highly organized. You can't add the cream to the sauce while trying to catch your three-year-old who is prancing naked round the kitchen. Nor can you make this type of sauce if you have to

69

scramble around in search of a clean bowl in which to decant the juice.

Temperamental sauces are not a slut's forte, but every so often it's worth the effort. The rule is to get everything laid out beforehand, including the children. Tying them to the bed or suspending them from the ceiling usually works. Lovers can be utilized to pass the gin and to wipe the sweat off your brow.

Horrible things can happen to difficult sauces, not the least of which is that they have a habit of 'catching' on the bottom of the pan and then tasting burnt. They also develop lumps just to spite you when you think you are home and dry. If the sauce lets you down, don't panic – get out your trusty packet of white sauce. It is better to serve a simple white sauce with parsley than to present a curdled or lumpy sauce with a burnt flavour.)

When you have added the eggs and cream to the broth, it will thicken immediately. Add the raisins and lemon juice. Reduce the heat to its lowest and drop in the walnuts of butter and flour. This will make the sauce even thicker and richer. Put the salmon on a dish. I remove the skin from the whole side of the fish so that people can more easily carve themselves thick steaks. Pour the sauce all over the fish and sprinkle with parsley.

With this dish I serve new potatoes and small peas on a separate plate.

Mackerel

I love mackerel. It has a rich, dark brown taste. It is also one of the cheapest fish you can buy, and again, so filling that you need little else except a salad and fruit to make a complete meal. I don't understand why anyone should want to make a sauce for this fish. Its taste is so strong that it would obliterate anything added to it.

6 mackerel	Salt and black pepper
1 oz butter	3 lemons
Flour	

Preheat oven to 375° F, gas mark 4.

Clean the mackerel thoroughly, then dredge them in

flour with salt and pepper added. Mackerel is a very fatty fish and needs only a little butter to cook it. Put all six fish into a wide oven-proof dish. Dot with butter and put it into the oven to cook for 40 minutes.

Again, it's as well to open them flat on to the plates before serving. I give each guest two large pieces of lemon to squeeze over the fish. It is also a good idea to put a big bowl in the middle of the table for people to throw the bones into.

a good idea to put
a Large bowl in the
middle of the table
to throw the bones into

Do have lots of paper towel rolls handy so that people can wipe their fishy hands, otherwise they will wipe them on the furniture or on each other. There is no point in having table napkins these days since paper towels are so much more convenient. Sluts are not afflicted with the need to martyr themselves to the chore of cleaning six disgusting table napkins the morning after. Sluts do, however, unlike slags, draw the line at newspaper or lavatory rolls.

Seafood Risotto

This is a very easy dish once you get used to the idea of frying the rice and then letting it cook in the juice from the mussels. Nine times out of ten you can throw the whole thing together and it will work. The tenth time, the rice lets you down and ruins the whole dish. If you are really worried, make the rice part the day before and just steam it when you are ready to add the shellfish and the vegetables. You can serve the risotto hot or, if you want it cold, add a strong French dressing while it is still hot and let it go cold at room temperature. The rice will absorb the French dressing, which is why the dressing needs to be extra strong. Hot or cold, this dish tastes delicious.

Most people think risottos are nothing but mounds of rice with a prawn or two hiding in the middle. Nothing is further from the truth, for true risottos are actually stuffed with goodies. If your risotto is as desolate as the Sahara desert, your recalcitrant guests will start looting each other's plates. Men have left their wives over risottos.

6 pints mussels	1 green pepper
1 lb prawns (peeled)	1 red pepper
1½ lb rice	3 cloves garlic
1 bottle medium dry white wine	4 tablespoons olive oil
	Salt and black pepper
1 bunch spring onions	Origan
3 large tomatoes	Black olives

72

Clean and cook the mussels as you would for *Moules marinière* (see pp. 57–8), only this time remove the beards yourself. If you don't soak the mussels overnight, do scrub them well under a running tap, otherwise the stock will be full of sand and you won't be able to hear yourself speak during the meal for the sound of gritted teeth.

Put the stock on one side and add the cooked, shelled mussels to the prawns. In a large saucepan put the olive oil, chopped spring onions (remember that the green tastes strongest, so don't cut it off) and garlic. Heat this and then add the rice, stirring until it is well covered. Add the stock gradually, cupful by cupful, until the rice has absorbed it all. If by any chance you have run out of stock before the rice is cooked, don't worry; just add more white wine. When it is nearly ready, cook the chopped tomatoes, green pepper, red pepper and black olives in a little olive oil until they are soft. Then add the mussels and the prawns. Use lots of black pepper, salt and origan. This dish should burst with good tastes. If you like, have a large bowl of grated cheese on the table and serve the dish with an interesting salad.

There are loads of extras you can add to the risotto. Try artichoke hearts from a tin, drained and quartered. Also experiment with tinned or fresh okra (lady's fingers) and a few chopped anchovies. The possibilities are countless.

Tuna Fish Pie

This is a delicious and filling dish. The problem is that, as it is made with milk, it will curdle if you cook it too fast. I always forget and put it in a hot oven, so it comes out looking like a horrible disease. When I get it wrong, I put masses of parsley all over it so that it looks like a luxurious swamp. Sometimes I use a tin of Nestlé's condensed milk which is less likely to curdle but is very rich. Actually the answer is to cook it long and slow. Do remember to slice the potatoes to a uniform thickness, otherwise some will be cooked and others raw. You can use a mandoline for this, which looks like an old-fashioned wooden washboard with a razor cunningly inserted in the middle. Drunken sluts had better watch out. (If worse comes to worst, slices of hand can always be served as fish fingers.)

2 tins tuna fish	2 oz butter
2 large onions	Parsley
6 large potatoes (peeled)	Grated cheese (optional)
1 pint milk	Salt and pepper to taste

Preheat oven to 335° F, gas mark 3.

Slice the onions and the potatoes into ¼-inch thick rounds. Drain the tins of tuna fish. Melt the butter in an oven-proof casserole, and layer the onions, tuna fish and potatoes until the ingredients run out. Finish with a layer of potato. Add the salt and pepper to the milk and put this over it.

Let the pie cook in a low oven for 2 hours. Take it out and, if you like, add cheese and put it under the grill. (I usually serve cheese separately, as I hate cooked cheese.) Sprinkle the dish with parsley – or, if the milk has curdled, *smother* it with parsley.

You can add almost any herb to this dish. I go through stages of cooking everything with origan or thyme. It is particularly good with sage.

Smoked Salmon and Potato Pie

You don't need to buy expensive smoked salmon for this dish. Most shops that sell smoked salmon have scrag ends wrapped up in greaseproof paper for posh pussies or marauding sluts.

½ lb smoked salmon in slivers	6 shallots, or a bunch of spring onions
1 pint white sauce (home-made or packet)	6 large potatoes
	2 oz butter
	10 large prawns

Preheat oven to 335° F, gas mark 3.

Melt the butter and fry the onions until they turn yellow. Don't let them cook too long or they will taste strong and ruin the delicate flavour of the dish. Layer the potato with slices of smoked salmon inserted here and there. Then pour the white sauce over it all. Cook it in a slow oven for about 1½ hours.

Decorate the top with the prawns, as otherwise it does look rather boring. Serve with peas.

Paella

Everyone who has been to Spain wants to tell you about his ultimate paella experience. Actually, they all make pigs of themselves on the paella, and then spend the rest of the holiday in the loo, clutching bottles of kaolin and morphine (liquid concrete). Apart from Spanish waiters, the other things to bring home are saffron, which is cheap out there, and Fundador (brandy).

Native Spanish paella can be quite dangerous, thanks to creatures such as the mussel. Mussels are civic-minded molluscs, and they spend much of their little lives cleaning up after the human race. Unfortunately, they have a merry sense of humour, and repay seafood enthusiasts with dire diseases like typhoid. Fortunately, the English sea is so cold that typhoid bacteria, and the English alike, avoid swimming in it. I avert disease when I am in hot countries by starting my day with a cup of coffee liberally laced with Fundador.

2 lb chicken	½ teaspoon powdered
1½ lb rice	saffron
¾ pint unshelled	¼ teaspoon paprika
prawns	Olive oil
4 tomatoes	Salt and black pepper
1 green pepper	3 cloves garlic
1 red pepper	Small tin artichoke
1 large onion	hearts

Into a paella pan (or a very large frying pan) pour enough oil to cover the bottom generously. Fry the chopped onion and the crushed garlic until brown, and then add the chicken cut into bite-sized pieces.

Good cooks can dismember a chicken without making it look as if a mass murder has taken place in the kitchen. I ask my butcher to do it for me. In the absence of a butcher, buy chicken pieces.

Fry the chicken for 12 minutes. Then add the tomatoes, quartered, and the green and red peppers cut into strips. Fish the whole lot out of the pan with a slotted spoon and put it to one side.

Swish 1½ lb of uncooked rice round in the oil, until all the grains are well coated. Then pour on 1½ pints of water to which you have added the saffron, salt, pepper and paprika. Excellent cooks get yer actual Spanish rice from Soho, but sluts stick to whatever brands they always use because rice is very unpredictable.

Now, put into the pan all the stuff you have laid aside and boil it for 15 minutes. By the end of this time a lot of the water should be absorbed. If it's too dry, add more water. If it's soggy, boil it very fast to dry it out. Taste a few grains at this point. They should still be a little chewy, because you want it to cook for 10 minutes more.

When you've adjusted the rice, add the unpeeled prawns and the cleaned mussels in their shells. Halve the artichoke hearts and add them as well. The shells of the prawns add very considerably to the taste of the paella.

If you are making this dish for the first time, plan to serve it cold so that you can mess about with the timing.

'Serve-themselves' Crabs

I never understand why everyone makes such a fuss about lobsters when to my mind crab has a much juicier, rounder taste and is not horribly expensive. Most people don't bother with crab because it's such an effort to clean, and the ready dressed shells taste of stale bread. Sluts serve them as they are. First of all, you go down to the fish shop and choose full, succulent crabs. Ask the fishmonger to open them for you, and look inside. If a crab is full of murky water, don't buy it; ask for another.

The English are amazingly cowardly about their right to buy decent food. They stand in queues looking pinched and miserable, and when it's finally their turn, they beg piteously for a few ageing scraps of food. No wonder shopkeepers despise their customers. There's no fun in selling to your average British consumer. On the Continent, people get their adrenalin flowing first thing in the morning by having a screaming match with the local grocer. The British are by comparison a passionless race.

Sluts, however, love food enough to insist on checking what they buy. Because they are prepared to argue, they get the best in the shop. It may take you a month or two to get your high street terrorized, but it's well worth doing. The good shops will love seeing you, and the bad shops will learn to hide under the counter or take to the hills upon seeing you, in which case you can serve yourself.

6 medium-sized crabs	Worcestershire sauce
3 lemons	Brown bread and butter
Mayonnaise	Salt and black pepper
Tomato ketchup	

Put your chopping board on the table, and collect all objects in the house that can be used to crack crab shells (e.g. hammers, nutcrackers, rolling pins, clogs, thick guests, etc.). Put two large bowls in the middle of the table to catch the debris from the crabs. Give each guest an opened crab and tell him to get on with it. If your fishmonger hasn't opened the crabs for you, stick a knife in at the back and lever it up until the base of the shell parts from the top half.

The only piece of advice you need to impart to the assembled table is that the grey spongy things round the inside, called 'dead man's fingers', must be removed. (If you're feeling in need of publicity, don't tell them and read all about it in the next day's papers. You can while away the hours in your cell by inserting their obituaries in *The Times*.) Squeamish guests will misunderstand the yellow stuff in the top of the shell. This is, of course, the most tasty part of the crab, and should be spooned out and spread on the brown bread and butter. If anyone baulks, tell them that this is all there is to eat, and take away their supply of alcohol. They will soon stop sulking and join in. It doesn't take long for people to get into the swing of things and to start hitting their crab and each other with hammers. I draw the line at pickaxes.

Put a big bowl of mayonnaise on the table, along with

COLLECT ALL Objects IN the HOUSE that can be used to CRACK CRAB SHELLS

tomato ketchup mixed with Worcestershire sauce. Also put out lots of lemon wedges. Crab is very rich, so I serve nothing but a large salad with it.

Cleaning up is easy if you put plenty of newspaper on the table before the meal. Cleaning up the guests is more difficult, but as this is a self-help meal, they can help themselves to your bathroom where they can help themselves to each other.

Sole with Parmesan Cheese

This is a quick and tasty fish dish, but it's not very filling on its own, so I serve it with rice.

6 fillets sole	½ oz butter
2 onions	Salt and pepper
1 green pepper	Parmesan cheese
4 tomatoes	
1 pint of Campbell's (or anyone else's) lobster soup	

Get your fishmonger to skin the sole for you. If he is in a foul mood use frozen fillets, because skinning fish is a time-consuming and laborious process. Use a large shallow oven-proof dish, and cook it on top of the stove or in the oven.

Melt the butter and fry the onions until they just turn colour. Add the green pepper and tomatoes and continue frying until these vegetables soften. Lay the fish or fillets gently on top of the vegetables and pour the lobster soup over everything. Add salt and pepper to taste, and let it simmer very gently for about 15 minutes. If you are not inviting me to dinner, you can sprinkle the cheese on top and put it under a hot grill or in a hot oven for 5 minutes to melt the cheese. Serve it with rice and wedges of lemon.

Fish Curry

There are endless kinds of curry to be found in English shops, from many Eastern countries, but I particularly like a curry paste from Thailand that is made from red chillis, onions, garlic, lemon grass, kaffir, lime peel, spices and shrimp paste. You can get this particular paste from a Chinese emporium just off the Kilburn Road in London. However, as Kilburn is not immediately available to everyone, there are numerous other alternatives. Madras curry powder is a very mild curry for those guests who do not possess asbestos mouths from years of overindulging in alcohol and fags. Fern's curry paste is another excellent curry found all over the country. Like all spices, it's a matter of experimenting until you find the taste you like. Sauce for this fish is well provided by a product called 'Fish Gravy', Han River Brand. It smells disgusting, but it's lovely with fish.

3 packets curry paste (or 2 tablespoons curry powder)	6 courgettes
	1 lb button mushrooms
	2 green peppers
6 cod fillets (skinned)	3 tablespoons fish sauce
1 pint milk	3 tablespoons vegetable
1 large aubergine	oil

Heat the oil and add the chopped aubergine, courgettes and green peppers. Fry until they are nearly cooked (about 15 minutes). Lift them out and put them to one side.

Put in the curry paste or powder, and mix it with the oil. Return the vegetables and add the milk. Simmer the mixture gently, and lower the cod fillets into the pan. Let it cook for a further 15 minutes, and serve it on a bed of rice.

If you make the curry too hot you can add yoghurt to the sauce, or put a bowl of yoghurt on the table for guests who wish to adjust the temperature for themselves.

FLESH

The Chinese think that we Westerners smell terrible because – they claim – we eat so much meat. I have not noticed that my vegetarian friends are any less malodorous than my carnivorous ones. I do feel, however, that it is much easier to use meat as part of a dish than to cook it as a roast with lots of accompanying side dishes.

Getting a roast to the table is a nightmare. It is either too rare and spurts blood all over the place or else it is overcooked and tastes like face flannels. There are of course such things as meat thermometers, but they seem to take a fiendish delight in misinformation. An alternative method of testing meat is to stick a long knife through the joint and see if the juices run clear; if they do, it's cooked. I don't take any chances: I carve a joint in the kitchen and put the slices on a heated plate. If I discover that it's undercooked, I put the slices in the gravy on top of the stove for a few minutes and they cook through. If it's overcooked, I do the same thing and let the gravy soften up the meat.

If by some miracle the meat is all right, I still carve it in the kitchen, because cutting thin slices of meat requires the kind of patience rarely possessed by a slut. An electric carving knife is a help. So is a patient lover. The problem is that carving knives tend to clog with grease and patient lovers sometimes make impatient sluts very angry. It is therefore wise for guests to stay out of the kitchen lest they witness a slut attacking a lover with a carving knife. Should the lover limp to the table bleeding, guests should inspect their meat with suspicion: sluts tend to be careless, and cannibalism is not one of life's great experiences.

81

GRAB a handful
and THROW it in

Even if you do manage to get the roast edible, another problem is co-ordinating all the vegetable dishes. I always dread a meal when I hear it's to be a roast, because it is bound to be served by an exhausted hostess with her hair lank with grease from the cooking. If she gets the meat hot, the vegetables are cold. If the vegetables are hot, the gravy is congealed. If, however, you do insist on serving up a roast, keep the vegetables simple. A very large baking dish can take the roast, potatoes and vegetables such as parsnips all in one go, thereby cutting out all the extra saucepans and saving you from running about frantically.

Sluts tend to use a lot of herbs and spices, partly to disguise their mistakes and partly because they can never follow a recipe that says 'add a small quantity'. This is usually translated as 'grab a handful and throw it in'.

The problem with requiring lots of different spices is that you end up with loads of little jars without labels full of mouldy bits of herbs. Poltergeists inhabit sluts' kitchens, so all those little spice racks wrench themselves out of the wall and smash on the floor. (It is easier to blame the poltergeists than to admit that you constantly overload the rack with jars that don't belong.) A solution for herbs is to buy already established potted herbs from your local nursery and put them in the bathroom. This way, the steam from the bath will keep the plants moist. Sluts do not remember to water things regularly, except for the back of their throats. Keep parsley, thyme, sage, rosemary and tarragon. If you keep them in the bathroom during the winter, they should thrive. If they don't and you have

the PROBLeM is that CARVING kNiveS tend to cloq with GReAse + that patient LoveRS sometimes Make IMPatient Sluts VeRy aNgRy

done your best, suspect the cats. It has to be explained very clearly to the cats that the plants are not inside to save them the trouble of going outside. If the cats don't listen, mine the pots with sticks. I lost a whole summer collection thanks to my cats.

the potAtoes are
NeARLY DoNe,
H aVe aNotHeR dRiNk eveRy-oNe

FuNNY SMELL?

Roast Lamb with Mustard Sauce

4 lb leg of lamb	1 tablespoon rosemary
4 cloves garlic	1 tablespoon thyme
1 oz butter	Salt and black pepper
¼ pint French mustard	1 teaspoon ginger
or Moutarde de Meaux	1 tablespoon olive oil
2 tablespoons soy sauce	1 oz butter

Sluts tend to follow the West Indian practice of inserting
garlic into deep holes in the meat. This makes the joint taste
of garlic right through. It is especially effective if the joint is
tough and tasteless. If, however, you can get excellent meat,
use the same method with fresh herbs. I have Lillypot Farm
nearby which sells the best lamb in London: it comes fresh
from Wales every day. For such lamb, too much garlic would
be a sin. However, this recipe is for any old leg of lamb.

Preheat oven to 350° F, gas mark 4.

Mix the mashed garlic with 1 oz of butter. Make slits in the
meat about every 3 inches. Using your fingers, force the
garlic deep into the meat. Now mix the mustard, soy sauce,

herbs, ginger and olive oil into a paste. Smear it all over the lamb. Put the lamb in the baking tray with olive oil. In order to make life easy, I put peeled and sliced parsnips round the roast because they taste delicious with the juice, or sliced green and red peppers. Roast for 1½ hours. I serve this dish with rice and peas.

If you want to serve it with roast potatoes, remember that they can be treacherous. Either they cook long before the roast and are as hard as bullets, or they come out white and flaccid. A useful tip is to rub the potatoes in a mixture of oil and flour. This helps to brown them. If you feel insecure about roasting potatoes, don't do it. Time and time again I have sat in drawing rooms getting faint with hunger while the hostess rushes in and out of the kitchen, pursued by clouds of black smoke, saying, 'The potatoes are nearly done. Have another drink everyone . . .' By the time they are done everyone is too far gone to care, except for the hostess who is trying to lever the potatoes off the baking tray while they obstinately refuse to let go.

Sluts tend to stick to baked potatoes. It's worth keeping six large nails around to put through them so that they cook right through more quickly, as the nails conduct the heat evenly throughout the potatoes. If you don't use nails, you run the risk of a subversive potato deciding to make a revolutionary protest by exploding all over the oven. The other hazard is that for some reason they take for ever to cook, and you end up having to remove most of the uncooked inside and fill the shells with Smash instant potato.

Beef Stew in Red Wine

Anything that involves stewing in sauces can be made the day before or even days before, and then heated up just before the guests arrive. Sluts tend to be easily distracted, so it's far better to get everything cooked the day before when the house is quiet than to try and organize it on the day, when the children have accidents in the garden and the dog has an accident all over the carpet. Most things taste better re-heated anyway, and if you make a mistake you have time to try again, instead of adding to your credit at the local take-away.

As sluts rarely bother with any form of socializing except for occasions involving food, they quite legitimately spend their money on first-class produce. Good stews need good wine. The idea that you can use a cheap, thin red wine for a good stew is wrong. A thin red wine will only make a thin red stew. Cheap red wine tastes like vinegar when cooked. For rich aromatic stews use a good bottle of Beaujolais, bottled in France. Your local Liquormart will have a good selection. Liquormarts specialize in left-over wines, and I always ask the manager to recommend a good bargain. Oddbins are another excellent source of cheap good wine.

3 lb lean stewing steak	Salt and pepper
8 oz bacon	2 tablespoons olive oil
1½ pints full red wine	1 tin tomato paste
1 tin consommé	2 carrots
2 cloves garlic	16 small shallots
1 tablespoon thyme	1 lb mushrooms
Flour	1 carton natural yoghurt

Preheat oven to 325° F, gas mark 2.

Put the oil into the bottom of the casserole and add the crushed garlic. Cut the bacon into 2-inch pieces, and fry until the fat runs.

Meanwhile dredge the meat, cut into 2-inch cubes, in the flour, to which you have added thyme, salt and pepper. Add the meat to the oil and swish it around until it is coated with oil. Add the peeled onions, diced carrots and tomato paste, and let it fry for about 5 minutes.

Pour the wine and a tin of beef consommé over the meat. Put it in the oven for 3–4 hours. About an hour before serving, add the mushrooms. I leave them whole. When you take the casserole from the oven, pour the carton of yoghurt over the top, and smother the whole thing with parsley.

Serve this stew with baked potatoes, rice or noodles. Noodles are the easiest of all. They take 5 minutes in boiling water. It's worth remembering to coat the pan with oil before boiling any sort of pasta so that it doesn't stick.

Beef and Beer

Beef cooked in beer has a marvellously rich taste. Try several types of beer and see how strong you like the taste. I use Ruddles County beer which you can get in your local off-licence. Occasionally I use Guinness, which gives the stew a very strong flavour and makes it look almost black.

For God's sake, remember to cut off any spare fat. Nothing is more off-putting than a mouthful of blubber and gristle. I can't remember how many times I have had to fish round my plate, hoiking out lumps of fat and then sticking them under my chair.

3 lb lean stewing beef	1 pint beer
3 large onions	½ pint beef stock
6 large carrots	4 cloves garlic
1 tablespoon brown sugar	1 tablespoon thyme
	Salt and pepper
2 tablespoons vinegar	

Preheat oven to 325° F, gas mark 2.

Get the butcher to slice the meat into large chunks for you. Start the casserole by heating it on top of the stove and letting the brown sugar caramelize. This means you get it hot enough to melt and go runny and then just begin to stick to the bottom of the pan. As soon as it does this, add 2 tablespoons of vinegar. The combined flavours will take away the bitter taste of the beer, and will give the stew a full, rich flavour.

Add the sliced onions and the garlic, and stir them round in the sauce. Then add the meat. If you are making a stew and want a thick gravy like the one in this recipe, do dredge the meat in flour before you put it into the casserole. (Non-sluts will also sear the meat first to keep in the juices; I prefer the juices in the gravy.) Once the chunks of meat have browned, add the sliced carrots and pour in the beer and the beef stock. Remember that a tin of beef consommé saves hours of effort.

Put the casserole in the oven for 2½ hours. Serve it with baked potatoes or rice, or new potatoes if they are around. Sluts never peel potatoes for boiling because they are too lazy. They serve them with the skins on. Anyone who dares to object is given a lecture on vitamins. If they are obstinate enough to continue to object, fix them with your beady eye and tell them they will get bowel cancer from lack of roughage. If that doesn't shut them up, proceed to describe the symptoms of bowel cancer in graphic detail. After that, they won't eat anything at all for the next few days.

Sluts love medical information, and they usually have a volume or two full of colour plates of revolting diseases. If things get dull, you can always get the book out. If things are really dire and no one looks like going home, show them one of the more lurid illustrations of venereal disease just before you serve Spotted Dick for pudding. This is guaranteed to clear the room.

Spanish Beef Stew

God knows why this is called Spanish Beef Stew; it's probably because there are tomatoes in it. It is cooked with white wine instead of the usual red, or you can use vermouth.

After throwing stews together for several years, you get a sort of universal stew. Sluts excel in producing these kinds of rich filling meals. Eventually, you get to the three-day stew. The first day you make a straightforward stew with loads of hearty vegetables and meat. Next day, you add beer or wine. Then after that, you curry what's left. If there is anything left over after that, put it on the garden to kill the weeds.

3 lb stewing steak	2 red peppers
¼ lb streaky bacon	¾ pint white wine
6 onions	½ pint beef stock
6 large tomatoes	3 cloves garlic
2 green peppers	3 tablespoons olive oil

Preheat oven to 325° F, gas mark 2.

The usual procedure: fry the garlic in the oil and add the onions, then add the stewing steak after dredging it in flour. Add green peppers, red peppers and the large tomatoes, having cut them all into quarters. Pour in the white wine and the beef stock, and put the casserole in the oven for 2½ hours.

I use a medium white wine for cooking, because if white

wine is dry it can taste too sharp. I serve this dish with spaghetti. Do remember to wipe the base of the pan with oil before boiling the spaghetti.

If you want to vary this dish, boil 1½ lb of rice and add it to the stew after 2 hours. Put the stew back into the oven for the extra half hour, and then serve it with a big bowl of grated cheese.

Chinese Beef Stew

3 lb stewing beef	3 cloves garlic
2 lb leeks	4 tablespoons sugar
3 large onions	½ teaspoon cinnamon
3 large carrots	½ teaspoon ginger
½ bottle sweet sherry	½ oz cornflour
¾ pint water	Black pepper and salt
3 tablespoons soy sauce	

Preheat oven to 325° F, gas mark 2.

Get the beef cut into 2-inch chunks. This time dredge the pieces in cornflour. Cornflour gives a slightly different texture to the stew than does plain flour.

Marinate the meat the night before by putting it in a bowl and pouring over the sherry, soy sauce, crushed garlic, sugar, cinnamon, ginger, salt and pepper. Leave it to soak until you are ready to cook. If you are a slut, you will probably forget to marinate the meat. Either you won't defrost it in time, or you won't get out of bed and get organized. Not to worry. A quick way out is to boil the ingredients of the marinade and drop the meat in for 2 or 3 minutes. You can do this with any dish that requires marinating if you are desperate.

Put the oil in the casserole. Fry the onions until they are brown. Add the drained meat and stir it around until the meat and onions are well covered. Cut the leeks into thick slices, using as much of the green stem as possible. Chop the carrots and add both vegetables to the stew. Add the marinade mixture at this point, and as it reheats, add the water. The liquid should cover the meat and vegetables; if it doesn't, add more water.

Cook for 2½ hours and serve with rice or noodles.

Veal in White Wine

3 lb veal	4 oz butter
1 lb tomatoes	3 cloves garlic
1 lb mushrooms	1 teaspoon thyme
½ lb courgettes	Black pepper and salt
4 onions	A bunch of parsley
¾ pint white wine	2 oranges
½ pint water	1½ lb rice

Preheat oven to 325° F, gas mark 2.

Get the veal cubed and dredge it in flour. Take the peel from half an orange and cut it into match sticks. Fry these sticks in the butter for a few minutes and then remove them. I chuck them away, saving the butter.

Chop the onions and fry them with the crushed garlic in the butter. This stew has quite a delicate taste, so cook the onions until they are golden, not brown, and then add the veal. Chop the tomatoes, mushrooms and courgettes and add them to the meat. Add the wine with the water, thyme, salt and pepper. Check that the liquid has covered the stew, and then add the juice of an orange.

Put the stew in the oven for 2½ hours. When you are ready to serve it, slice the remaining orange very thinly and decorate the top of the stew with orange slices and parsley. Serve with rice or boiled potatoes.

Beef and Potato Hot Pot

Hot pots are traditionally served in the north of England on cold winter nights. There are many different versions, and as many cooks who will insist that theirs is the only version. Actually, as the dish was the staple meal of the poor, the most authentic version was probably the one that included stray cats and the odd rat or two. This stew should have a really thick gravy.

3 lb stewing steak	1 pint water
3 lambs' kidneys	2 oz cooking lard or oil
3 large onions	
8 carrots	2 oz flour
6 large potatoes	Salt and pepper
2 pints beef stock	4 bay leaves

The traditional hot pots usually contained kidneys. The problem with the cheap kidneys, like ox or pigs', is that they tend to taste of pee. You can get the taste out by rinsing them in a bowl of vinegar and water. If the smell is ferocious, use straight vinegar. Lambs' kidneys are the best, unless you particularly like a strong kidney taste as I do. I use pigs' kidneys.

If you are squeamish, get your friendly butcher to split the kidneys open and take out any stray tubes or other debris. Sluts tend to be very anal about food, and actually enjoy dissecting offal. Most guests don't want a blow by blow account of how one prepares kidneys or how to jug a hare in its own blood. Neither do those who are not on the floor in a dead faint want to listen to a lecture on the alienation of man from nature. However, it's all very interesting information, and even if the adults don't want to listen, you will find a rapt audience in their children.

Preheat oven to 325° F, gas mark 2.

Cut the kidneys and the beef into bite-sized portions and dredge them in the flour. Slice the onions, carrots and potatoes into fairly thick rounds, because this dish is cooked slowly; if you dice them too thin, they will disintegrate. Use a large casserole and fry the meat in the bottom of the casserole with a few onions. Turn the meat and onions over until they are covered in oil or cooking fat and are brown.

Remove the meat and start layering all the ingredients. Start with onions, then put a layer of beef and kidney, followed by a layer of carrots, and then potatoes. Add salt and pepper to taste, and several bay leaves. Keep layering until you run out of ingredients. Then put a final layer of potato on top. Pour 2 pints of stock over the lot, and stick it in the oven for 2½ hours. Check after 2 hours and see if it has dried out. If it has, put more stock in. If it's too wet, pour extra juice out. Take the lid off for the final half hour.

The stock can be made from any of the well-known gravy mixes. Bisto is particularly good for this kind of dish. Perfectionists can make their own, or you can stick to tins of consommé.

The pleasure of this dish, apart from its simplicity, is the fact that it avoids the washing-up of lots of pots and pans. If your guests don't seem to be the type who readily leap to the kitchen for washing-up duty, or if you are in between lovers, I suggest you play 'peasants' – a very exotic ethnic family game in which everyone has a spoon and eats out of the same pot. If you find that you have accidentally invited a sociologist, you may as well let him deliver a lecture and get right down to drinking straight out of the bottle. The local letch will probably suggest that you all remove your clothes and wear blankets like in the old days. Encourage him at all costs, so that you can nick all the clothes and sell them at the local second-hand shop to cover the cost of the meal.

Pork and Beans

This is a very filling dish. As children are fond of saying, 'Beans means fartz', and if you don't soak the beans enough by the time you serve coffee, the assembled company can sound like the Royal Philharmonic on a bad day. If everyone is well acquainted, it can be a source of amusement, but if people are there for the first time, it can be unnerving to find that the delicate little girl on your left sounds like the cannon in the 1812 Overture. If it suits your perverse sense of humour to watch your guests struggle with that age-old problem of how to break wind in company while retaining social poise, serve the beans and sit back after you have taken a teaspoon of bicarbonate of soda to insulate yourself. If, however, you wish to make the evening less festive, put the bicarbonate of soda in the casserole and use 'party poppers' instead.

Sluts fart quite happily, and graciously acknowledge the event. Others take evasive action and pretend it was the next-door neighbour or the cat. Either way, I recommend the painter Salvador Dali's brilliant paper on 'The Art of Farting' from his book *Diary of a Genius*. This gives you plenty of opportunity to read out hilarious passages to the guests and to observe who is shtupping whom by their lack of embarrassment at each other's trumpeting. If you add wine to the dish, double the soda bicarbonate, because the alcohol will ferment with the beans and will double the volume of sound. Elijah was the first prophet to discover self-propelled ascension. The flaming chariot was probably kept alight by methane gas.

2 lb white haricot beans	3 onions
1½ lb belly of pork	4 tablespoons olive oil
1½ lb breast of lamb	6 bay leaves
¼ lb bacon	Thyme
¾ lb garlic sausage	Parsley
3 cloves garlic	Salt and pepper

Soak the beans overnight. If you remember, change the water a couple of times; this helps to remove the slightly bitter taste of the beans. This is a large dish to cook because the beans take up so much space, so you will need a very big casserole, at least 6 inches deep by 12 inches across.

Get the butcher to chop up the belly of pork, the breast of lamb and the bacon into pieces for you. Chop the boiling sausage into 2-inch rings. In the traditional recipe, all the meats would be buried whole in the beans. The recipe would include goose, and sometimes half a duck, but it's an awful struggle serving all the different meats once they are cooked. Sluts will find this recipe far easier and just as tasty.

Preheat oven to 325° F, gas mark 2.

Fry the onions and the garlic in the bottom of the casserole until they brown. Add the meats, and stir them until they are coated with the onion juice and oil.

Add the bay leaves, thyme and pepper to taste. Now add the beans and gently mix them into the meats until the beans are evenly distributed. Pour water over the beans until they are just covered, and put the casserole into the oven for 5 hours. Make sure the lid fits tightly, otherwise the stew will dry out. Half an hour before serving, take the dish out and check the seasoning. It should have formed a crust of beans. If it has, it's ready to serve. If it hasn't, put the oven on high and stick it back for half an hour with a layer of breadcrumbs over the beans.

Serve the dish at the table, covered with parsley. Don't add the salt until the end of the cooking, or the beans will never soften.

Chinese Spare Ribs

This is an 'up to the elbows in grease' dish. It is extremely hard to get good, meaty spare ribs in this country. Sometimes a butcher will produce a few bleached looking bones and insist they are spare ribs or a rather lank-looking version of lamb chop. Take him to task, and insist on a large, well-covered spare rib. Remind him that Sampson did his smiting with the jawbone of an ass, and you can be just as lethal with the nearest legbone of a lamb if he doesn't co-operate. Harrods still sell the best spare ribs in the country at a reasonable price. The reason why butchers don't much like selling spare ribs is that there is not much money for them in doing so. But if your butcher is a true friend, he will make sure you get the best.

6 good-sized spare ribs for each person	4 cloves garlic
	1 bottle soy sauce
3 large onions	1 jar ginger in syrup

In a large baking tray, mix together the sliced onions, chopped garlic, the contents of a small jar of ginger with syrup and the soy sauce. Put the spare ribs in this marinade the night before the meal, and turn them over first thing the next morning.

An hour and a half before you want to eat the ribs preheat the oven to 550° F, gas mark 9, and cook the ribs for an hour. If you want to make life easy for yourself, put large potatoes in to bake when you put the oven on. Otherwise serve the spare ribs with rice or noodles.

Kidneys in Tomato Sauce and Red Wine

12 lambs' kidneys	1 medium tin tomato paste
6 rashers bacon	
3 onions	¾ pint red wine
¾ lb button mushrooms	Salt and pepper
1 large tin Italian plum tomatoes	Thyme, basil, or rosemary to taste

Preheat oven to 325° F, gas mark 2.

Slice the lambs' kidneys into 2-inch pieces and fry gently

with the onion, garlic and bacon pieces. For this recipe, it is better to dice the onions rather than slice them; this will give the casserole a firmer texture.

When the kidneys have browned, add the mushrooms and coat everything with the oil. Mix the tomato paste with the tin of plum tomatoes plus a teaspoon of brown sugar. The brown sugar will take away the slightly bitter taste from the tomatoes and red wine, which can ruin a dish. Pour in the red wine. Add salt and pepper to taste, and the herbs: thyme, basil or rosemary are excellent for this dish. If you are lucky you may be able to get some French tarragon, which gives the dish a unique flavour. Tarragon is very strong, and should not be used with other herbs. Cook for about 40 minutes.

Serve this dish on a bed of rice with spaghetti or noodles. Peas or courgettes go well with it. I use frozen sliced courgettes: pour boiling water over them and let them boil quickly for a few minutes. Remove them and drain off the juice. Put 2 oz butter and the juice of 2 lemons into the pan and return the courgettes. Keep them warm until you are ready to serve them.

Instant Greek Casserole

Most sluts have an affinity for anything Greek – particularly Greek men. There is an ancient fable that tells of the dissolution of the twelve tribes of Judah. Actually, there were thirteen, and members of the thirteenth tribe were known as the Hyperboreans. They were the mystics, poets and painters, and the ne'er-do-wells of all the tribes. They made their home in Greece among the islands, and were known 'to live at the back of the North wind', hence the name. Sluts recognize the address instantly, and fellow sluts feel an immediate kinship with each other. We sluts were all Hyperboreans, and our real home is in Greece. Just a sniff of basil, the sound of a bazouki and the memory of a Greek blue sea can transport us far away from the day-to-day problems of living and into the magic timelessness of a Greek island.

My island is Zakinthos, and my Greek family is the Milonas family who own a perfect headland where I camp every summer. Mama Gina makes this dish properly, and I often cheat. Here are both versions:

12 vine leaves	3 cloves garlic
1½ lb rice	3 tablespoons olive oil
3 onions	Basil or thyme to taste
4 large ripe tomatoes	Black pepper and salt
1 large tin tomatoes	

I buy fresh vine leaves from Adamou's. Most Greek or Cypriot delicatessens have them. If not, buy the packet variety. Either way you must soak them in several changes of water or they will be as tough as old Greek slippers.

Cook the rice. Add plenty of basil, salt and black pepper. Make the rice into little mounds and put each mound in the middle of a vine leaf. Fold the edges of the leaf over until it looks like a little GPO parcel.

When you have done all twelve vine leaves, take a break and have a drink. If you hate the idea of messing about with vine leaves, give them to your lover in place of Marks and Spencer knickers, and buy for yourself two tins of dolmades, which are stuffed vine leaves.

Preheat oven to 325° F, gas mark 2.

Into the bottom of a casserole put 3 tablespoons of olive oil. Crush the garlic and let it fry until it goes brown. Add the roughly chopped onions and fry them until they start to turn yellow. Remove the onions and fry the tomatoes, which you have quartered, until they are coated with oil (about 4 minutes). Remove everything and start again.

Put the onions back in the bottom, then the stuffed vine leaves with the tomatoes covering them. Put the rest of the onions on top. Pour a large can of Italian tinned tomatoes into the casserole. If this does not just cover the mixture, add a little water. Put the casserole into the oven for 2 hours, and serve with a Greek salad (see p. 44) and pitta bread. A large plate of black olives goes well with this dish, and I usually serve Demestica, a Greek wine which again you will find at your Greek or Cypriot deli.

If you want to make this dish even more filling, add 1 lb minced lamb to the stuffing for the vine leaves in place of rice. Use ½ lb cooked rice to help glue the mince together.

If you do use meat, it's well worth tying up the little parcels with string, as the meat tends to try and escape. There is nothing more unsightly than deflated vine leaves covering a soggy pond of minced lamb.

Stuffed Aubergines

This is a very well-known dish all over the Middle East. Now that we have aubergines in the shops all year round, it is worth exploring ways of serving this excellent vegetable. Aubergines are sometimes known as 'poor man's meat', and they are indeed so rich and filling that you can see why good cooks and poor peasants often substitute aubergines for meat. There is a legend that aubergines planted in your garden can lead to female sterility, which is good news for the local family-planning clinic. The Imaman, who was a Turkish holy man, was supposed to have fainted upon being served this dish. Whether this was from delight at the taste, or the news of his wife's infertility, or the size of the bill, we shall never know.

2½ lb mince	Origan to taste
3 onions	1½ lb rice
6 large aubergines	3 oz raisins
1 medium tin tomato concentrate	3 cloves garlic
1 large tin tomato juice	3 tablespoons olive oil
	Black pepper and salt

The difficulty with aubergines is how to scoop out the inside without doing the vegetables or yourself an injury. The simplest method is to cut them lengthwise and then scoop out the middle with a teaspoon. Put the aubergine shells into a bowl of salt water for at least an hour to get rid of the bitter taste. Take them out and dry them. They are now ready for stuffing.

Minced meat must be well seasoned or else it tastes terrible. It must also be made from good lean meat, otherwise it leaks rancid fat everywhere. So get the best mince from your butcher. The seasoning is according to your own taste, so keep munching as you go along. If the meat seems boring and tasteless, add some more spice. Mince needs lots of spicing, far more than recipes usually allow for.

Crush the garlic and fry it in a frying pan with the olive oil. Chop the onions finely and brown them with the garlic. Add the mince and fry it for about 5 minutes, stirring constantly. Take the fried ingredients off the stove and add the tin of tomato concentrate, spoon by spoon, until you have a thick mixture that will fill the aubergine shells. If for some reason there is not enough tomato paste, add water, but it is important to go slowly as the stuffing can become horribly sloppy if you are not careful.

Put the shells into a baking tray or oven-proof casserole which has been well oiled to prevent the shells sticking. Fill the cases with the mince mixture and pour tomato juice between the shells to a depth of about 1½ inches. Put the casserole into a low oven (325° F, gas mark 2) for 1½ hours.

Cook the rice with the raisins. If you feel like being extravagant, add some pine nuts which are horribly expensive but give a nice crunch and taste of pine trees. Dust the aubergines with parsley and serve with the rice. If the aubergines dry out, you can always moisten them with a tablespoon or more of yoghurt.

Chilli con Carne

This is a very hot and spicy dish. Bicarbonate of soda is also needed here for the same reasons described in a preceding recipe. Again, it is a Mexican peasant dish, originally made with lumps of passing horses which were too slow to get away in time. If the thought of ambushing lame mares doesn't grab you, I recommend that you use stewing steak. Steak, however, requires a lot more effort than mince, because you have to soak the beans and stew the meat before you can get the casserole on the road. I do it the easy way and use mince and chilli sauce. The virtuous use stewing beef and grind their own chilli powder.

1½ lb red kidney beans	4 cloves garlic
3 lb mince	Origan, cumin
1½ pints beef stock or	Chilli sauce
consommé	4 tablespoons olive oil
3 large onions	Salt and black pepper

Soak the beans overnight. Change the water several times. Into a large casserole put 4 tablespoons of olive oil, and fry the crushed garlic. Add the roughly chopped onions and continue to fry until the onions are brown. Put in the minced meat and stir it round until it has browned. Add 1½ tablespoons of origan and cumin mixed, and chilli sauce to your liking. Check the taste and add more if you like. Add salt and pepper and check again.

Add the beef stock to the casserole and simmer it for 1½ hours on top of the stove. Keep an eye on it, and if it looks as if it's going to dry out, add more water. Just before serving, taste to see if it is spicy enough. If it is too hot, which is always possible when using chilli sauce or powder, add yoghurt and put a bowl of yoghurt on the table. If you really get it wrong, leave a bucket of water by the table to extinguish burnt guests. The problem with eating very hot, spicy dishes is that, like candles, you can get burnt at both ends.

Meat Loaf

This dish is only as good as the filling for the loaf. If the mince is dry and boring, the whole thing is a disaster. So it's worth taking time over the mixture. If you get it right, the fried bread round the filling is excellent.

1 large loaf of bread or 2 small ones	½ lb chopped mushrooms
2 lb mince	1½ tablespoons sage
3 onions	3 cloves garlic
1 green pepper	Salt and pepper
1 red pepper	

Preheat oven to 325° F, gas mark 2.

Cut off one end of a large, crusty loaf. Scrape out the inside of the loaf but don't make holes in the shell. Try not to leave any breadcrumbs, because they will go all soggy.

Fry the garlic and the finely minced onions in the oil until they brown. Then add the chopped red and green peppers. Add the mince and fry gently, adding the mushrooms, then the sage, salt and pepper to taste.

When it is all well covered in oil, spoon it into the shell

of the loaf. It is necessary to tie the sliced end of the loaf back on with string, and sit it in a baking tray lined with foil. Brush oil over the whole loaf and sprinkle it lightly with thyme or origan. Put it into the oven for an hour, then turn the oven up to 450° F, gas mark 6, for a further half hour. Have a look at it before you get it out. It should be crisp and brown. If it isn't, roast it a little longer. Serve it with parsley, boiled potatoes and a salad.

AND FOWL

I like cooking chicken dishes best of all. Unfortunately, I am also very fond of chickens. I never understand why people are so rude and disparaging about the lifestyle of this fine bird. My dream of a cottage in the country always includes a batch of chickens strolling around the house, clucking at each other. I plan to awake every morning to the sound of triumphant hens laying perfect brown eggs for my breakfast. The only problem with this dream is that I am incapable of killing anything, so the cottage would soon be overrun by a huge gang of geriatric fowl.

Many people are squeamish about handling birds. Indeed, there is something very unseemly about sticking your hand into the gaping orifice of a dead fowl and pulling out handfuls of entrails. How you feel about it depends on how you see yourself. Sluts have no problem with blood and guts, unlike their faint-hearted sisters.

Such delicate members of the female sex are inclined to have names like Moira or Elinore, and their lovers are the huge, hearty mugger type. Sluts serve them the 'parson's nose' if they are High Church, or the 'pope's nose' if they are Catholic. Either way, the poor girl is far too well-bred to refuse to eat this conspicuously revolting morsel. Her rugger-bugger of a lover finds it all a great laugh and slaps her encouragingly on the back in between telling lewd chicken jokes. If the slut sits back, the delicate guest will choke and her lover will burst a blood vessel with laughter, thereby clearing the room of their unwanted company. Any cool slut finding herself the guest of a malevolent hostess who has put the parson's nose on her plate knows how to handle the situation well. She thanks the hostess profusely and then picks up the offending piece and deposits it lovingly on her neighbour's plate along with a generous smile of goodwill. Mind you, chicken is to some people what liver was to Portnoy, but who's complaining?

If I am going to cook a delicate chicken dish, I use a free-range chicken. Frozen ones are to be used only for curries or thick stews because unless they are heavily disguised they taste of fish. If I roast a chicken, I cook the stuffing separately and fill the cavity with butter mixed with garlic and rosemary. This keeps the chicken very moist during cooking, and the herbs permeate the flesh deliciously.

Roast Chicken and Lemons

1 large roasting chicken	2 cloves garlic
6 large leeks	½ teaspoon rosemary
6 small parsnips	Salt and black pepper
3 lemons	to taste
½ lb butter	

Preheat oven to 425° F, gas mark 7.

Use a large oven-proof dish which can take the chicken and the vegetables. Crush the garlic and mix it with ¼ lb butter, and add the rosemary. Smear the rest of the butter over the chicken and sprinkle flour over the whole bird. Peel the parsnips and the leeks. Put the chicken in the baking dish and surround it with the vegetables.

Cut the lemons in half. Put one half inside the chicken and squeeze the others over the vegetables, and chuck the skins into the dish.

Cook for 1 hour, then have a look and see how all is progressing. If the skin is brown, baste it with the juices

102

and lower the oven to 325° F, gas mark 2, for another half hour. If you are worried that it is not properly cooked, take it out and cut down the joint of the thigh. You can then see if it is at all pink. If it is, turn the oven up to 550° F, mark 9, for the last half hour. If you do need to do this, cover the breast with foil.

Until you are really acquainted with your oven you are likely to find that cooking times will be inaccurate however closely you follow the instructions. The main thing is not to panic. If the bird is raw, keep cooking. If it is horribly overcooked, carve it in the kitchen and simmer it in the gravy for a further 10 minutes. Sluts tend to get roasting times wrong because they never remember to defrost until just before they are ready to cook. Then they throw the bird into the oven, forgetting to remove the plastic pack from the inside. They usually remember when they smell the plastic melting. However, once they have prised the entrails from the partially frozen carcass, they swear on a bottle of Gordon's to remain true to fresh fowls.

The lemons give the chicken a lovely fresh taste, and the vegetables absorb the juices. I sometimes vary this dish by adding a tin of Italian plum tomatoes to the gravy and serving it with rice instead of roast potatoes.

...YOURS, I BELIEVE.

aNY cool slut finding HeRseLf the guest of a MaLevoLaNt hostess who has put the PaRsoN's NosE oN HeR PLaTe KNows how to haNdLe the situatioN well

Drunken Chicken

This is a favourite slut recipe. I last cooked it in Spain in a sparse little villa where I had to use a suitcase as my kitchen table. Still, I was blissfully happy because it was April and all the best food was in plentiful supply. It is a shame that we all are prone to take our holidays in August when the heat has dried out the local food, and the demand is such that we are usually offered imported goods. This particular year it rained the whole time I was there, but the artichokes were the size of fingernails and the wild asparagus was just coming into season. I cooked all day, and we ate gargantuan meals washed down with rough wine and mellow Spanish brandy.

6 chicken pieces	¼ cup whisky
1 lb mushrooms	¼ cup kirsch
3 chopped onions	2 egg yolks
4 cloves garlic	2 cups cream
¾ cup port	½ lb butter
½ cup brandy	Salt and black pepper

Preheat oven to 350° F, gas mark 3.

Use good meaty chicken pieces. The trouble with frozen chicken pieces is that they are tough and stringy. This recipe needs succulent chicken because the tenderer it is the more the booze will be absorbed.

Dredge the chicken pieces in flour. In a large casserole melt ¼ lb of butter. Chop the onions and garlic, and fry them until they are golden brown. Add the mushrooms, diced. Pour in all the alcohol and allow to simmer for 10 minutes. Put the casserole in the oven for 1 hour.

Meanwhile, break 2 egg yolks into a bowl and beat them until they are frothy. Add 2 cups of cream, salt and black pepper to taste. Put 3 tablespoons of the chicken juice slowly into the egg mixture and then return the sauce to the casserole. Don't let it boil or it will curdle. Simmer it slowly on top of the stove. Smother it in parsley, and serve with baked potatoes and peas.

SLUTS RAther Like this PASTiMe — it Makes one feel SO RURAL

SLUTS NEVER PANIC, they get dRUNK

Chicken and Beans

This recipe is excellent for a cold winter's evening. All warnings about social repercussions have already been given in the last chapter (see Pork and Beans).

6 chicken pieces	4 cloves garlic
6 thick slices garlic sausage	4 tablespoons olive oil
2 lb red kidney beans	Salt and pepper to taste
3 onions	Parsley, thyme, origan

You need a deep casserole for this recipe. If you can find a Spanish bean pot, so much the better. These are made of brown glazed clay and look as if they were pregnant. The belly is huge, then the pot narrows up to a small neck with a lid. They don't cost much in Spain and they are even cheap here. This is partly because they break very easily, but they do look amazingly good in the middle of the table, and the shape makes sure that the heat is spread evenly through the beans.

Soak the beans overnight. Change the water the next morning and at lunchtime.

Preheat oven to 325° F, gas mark 3.

Dredge the chicken pieces in seasoned flour. Chop and fry the onions and garlic, and add them to the casserole which is bubbling with olive oil. Add the chicken pieces and stir. Add the garlic-flavoured boiling sausage and then the beans. Mix until everything is coated in oil. Add enough water just to cover all the ingredients, and put it in the oven for 3 hours.

If by any chance you haven't remembered to soak the beans, use tinned kidney beans. I have, in moments of desperation, been known to cook this dish in half an hour in a high oven with tinned beans, precooked chicken and dried onions. As with most things, a reduction in the standard of cooking can be compensated for by an increase in the quantity of alcohol. If you have to resort to instant cooking, try a before-dinner drink called a 'leg-opener', a mixture of vodka and amaretto – a very potent drink. After several rounds of these, people's taste buds are anaesthetized and their minds are on other things.

Chicken and Coconut

This is easy and quick to make. Coconut gives a lovely flavour to chicken.

6 chicken pieces	½ block coconut cream
4 large onions	or 1 packet desiccated
1½ lb tomatoes or 1½	coconut
tins plum tomatoes	1 teaspoon cayenne
4 cloves garlic	pepper
	Salt and pepper

In a large casserole brown the pieces of chicken with the chopped onions and garlic. Take the pieces out and put them to one side while you make a tomato sauce with quartered tomatoes. This involves letting them cook gently until they collapse in a mushy heap. If they are not suf- ficiently juicy to make their own sauce (this will depend on the type of tomatoes you use) moisten the mixture with a little chicken stock or water.

Put the chicken pieces back into the casserole and simmer them for ¼ hour. Now melt the coconut block in a small saucepan over a low heat. If you do not live near a shop that sells creamed coconut in half-pound blocks that look like butter, use desiccated coconut (soak the packet overnight in a pint of water and use the juice). To the creamed coconut add sufficient water to make up 1 pint of liquid, then add this liquid to the casserole. Add the salt, pepper and cayenne to taste, and simmer the whole thing for a further half hour.

I serve this dish with rice and peas.

Chicken in Wine

Like so many other dishes, chicken stewed in wine is a classic recipe all over southern Europe. Originally, very poor peasants would stew their very stringy chickens in wine to soften the meat and add a rich taste to what would otherwise have been a very gamey experience. All cooks have their own version of this traditional dish. Provided you use a good bottle of red wine and cook the chicken slowly, not much can go wrong unless you have forgotten to kill the chicken. Don't be put off by posh people going on about the *coq-au-vin* they had in Bordeaux. Let them yammer on about the different types of smoked bacon or pickled goose that must be added to the casserole to make it a success. Remember, good cooking is like good sex: those who enjoy it don't have to brag about it all the time.

6 large chicken pieces	1½ bottles good red wine (Burgundy)
1 packet streaky bacon	
12 small shallots	1 miniature (2 tablespoons) brandy
¾ lb button mushrooms	
¼ lb butter	Origan to taste
4 cloves garlic	Salt and black pepper

Leaving the onions whole, fry them and the garlic in butter in the casserole. Cut the bacon into bite-sized pieces and

anything alcoholic
that's close to a
slut's hand, tends
to go down her throat

add them to the onions and garlic. Keep it all frying for about 10 minutes.

Add the chicken pieces, having first dredged them in flour. Coat the chicken with the juices from the bacon and vegetables. Add the button mushrooms.

At this point, if you have brandy to hand (which is unlikely because anything alcoholic that's close to a slut's hand tends to go down her throat) you can amuse yourself by setting light to the whole casserole. The idea behind this is not as daft as it seems, as I've already explained: the fire will burn off the fat, leaving the dish less greasy as well as adding an extra dimension to the taste of the casserole. If you feel like making the effort, remember to heat the brandy in a saucepan before you light it. Set light to it in the saucepan and pour it while it is still flaming over the chicken. Once the flames have died down – and assuming you have not set light to the kitchen or your eyebrows – add the bottle of red wine.

Let the casserole simmer for at least 3 hours on top of the stove. Keep it well covered so that the liquid does not evaporate. Just before serving, taste it and add salt, pepper and origan to your liking. You will find it so rich that it won't need much spicing.

I usually serve this dish with rice or new potatoes if they are in season. Sometimes I add ½ pint of single cream just before serving, or the same amount of yoghurt. Most sluts are such dreadfully messy servers that they tend to use chicken pieces rather than a whole chicken. It is preferable to use the whole chicken because you get far richer gravy from the carcass than you do from a few chicken bones. However, you must balance that gain against the awful struggle of dismembering the chicken when most of it tends to migrate to the ceiling.

Chicken in Tarragon

This dish is very like the previous recipe except that you use white wine and different vegetables. It does not take so long to cook either, as the sauce is much lighter.

6 large chicken pieces	¼ lb butter
3 large onions	1 bottle dry white wine

1 lb carrots	½ pint cream
8 celery stalks	6 sprigs tarragon
¾ lb button mushrooms	Salt and black pepper to taste

Tarragon has a very strong taste all of its own. You can buy French tarragon in pots from good nurseries like Crabtree Gardens in Crabtree Lane, Fulham. It is a very pretty plant and is delicious with fish and chicken or in salads. Again, how much to use is up to you. Sluts always spice everything heavily. In this recipe I use more tarragon than many people would probably enjoy. The answer is to start the dish with half the amount, and to taste it at the end. If you feel it needs more, add it. Remember, you can always make a dish stronger, but once the spices are in, you're stuck with it. The only way to make a dish milder is to add yoghurt. If it is too late and even yoghurt makes it taste like a dish fit only for Attila the Hun, try it on the children or curry it.

Thinly slice the onions, carrots, celery and mushrooms. Dredge the chicken pieces in the flour. Fry the vegetables in butter in the casserole, stirring until they soften (about 10 minutes). Add the chicken and let it turn pale yellow (again, about 10 minutes). Put the tarragon sprigs in with the salt and black pepper.

Add the wine and turn the stove down so that the casserole just simmers. Let it cook slowly for a further hour. Take it off and taste it. Adjust the seasoning and then pour in ½ pint of cream. Make sure you take the casserole off the stove first so that it comes off the boil, otherwise it will curdle and look disgusting. If it does, remember my advice from previous dishes. Don't panic – get out the candles. Low lights and lots of parsley disguise most mistakes.

Orange and Lemon Chicken

I don't like the Australian habit of festooning meat with fruit, but certain fruits do have an affinity with certain meats. Apricots are delicious with pork and pineapple goes well with ham. This dish is nice on·a summer evening because it is light and pretty to look at.

111

6 large chicken pieces
6 leeks
½ lb baby courgettes
1 green pepper
1 red pepper
¼ lb butter
¼ pint unsweetened
  orange juice

¼ pint stock or
  consommé
¼ pint sweet vermouth
1 orange
1 lemon
Salt and black pepper to
  taste

Dredge the chicken pieces in flour. Cut the leeks into 2-inch pieces and slice the green and red peppers. If the courgettes are small enough, leave them whole; if not, cut them in half. Melt the butter in the casserole and add the vegetables. Stir them gently until they soften, then add the chicken pieces and coat them with the butter and juices (about 10 minutes).

Pour in ¼ pint of orange juice, ¼ pint of chicken stock or consommé, and ¼ pint of sweet vermouth. Add salt and pepper to taste. Let the casserole simmer for 1 hour. Just before serving, add the juice of half a lemon. This takes away the slightly sweet taste of the orange and vermouth. Slice the rest of the lemon and the orange and decorate the top of the casserole with the pieces. Watercress mixed with the sliced fruit looks very pretty. I serve this casserole with tagliatelle.

Chicken, Peas and Rice

This is a traditional West Indian dish. There are very many different ways of cooking it: Cleo, my daughter, learned this version from her mother-in-law who comes from Jamaica. Each island has different methods of spicing. Russler, my adopted son who comes from Granada, adds curry powder to the marinade. For his version, see below.

6 chicken pieces
3 onions
3 cloves garlic
1 tablespoon thyme
1 tablespoon black
  pepper

2 tablespoons tomato
  sauce
1 chicken-flavoured
  Oxo cube
1½ lb rice

112

1 teaspoon onion salt	1 lb gunga peas or red
1 teaspoon garlic salt	kidney beans
1 lemon	Shredded cabbage
3 tablespoons corn oil	1 small bottle
¼ bottle soy sauce	mayonnaise
1½ pints water	

Cleo starts the dish by marinating the chicken pieces over-night. She slices 3 onions into thin rings and crushes the cloves of garlic. She then adds the thyme, black pepper, onion salt and garlic salt. She puts the whole lot into a bowl and adds the juice of a lemon. An hour before she is ready to eat, she fries the chicken pieces in 3 tablespoons of oil and adds more oil if needed, but is careful not to use too much.

When the pieces are completely fried, she removes them and puts them aside. She scrapes all the juices and herbs from the sides of the casserole and adds the soy sauce and then the water. She crumbles an Oxo cube into the water, and when it is simmering she adds 3 tablespoons of tomato sauce. She then sprinkles flour into the gravy, and she assures me it never lumps. Mine always does, so I stick to mixing it with butter. She returns the chicken pieces to the gravy and lets it cook for as long as it takes to boil the rice and gunga peas.

Soak the gunga peas (or red kidney beans if you can't get gunga peas) overnight. Throw away the water and replace it with fresh water to cover the now swollen peas. Pour the water and peas into a saucepan and add the rice. Cook for about 20 minutes, boiling furiously without a lid. Watch to see it doesn't dry out; add more water if there is any danger. After 20 minutes, take it off the heat and put it aside to steam for 10 minutes with the lid on.

In Russler's version, you leave out the Oxo cube and the tomato sauce. He starts the dish by sprinkling 3 table-spoons of brown sugar on the bottom of the casserole. He lets is melt until it just begins to caramelize. When it is bubbling, he 'cuts' it, as he calls it, with 3 tablespoons of malt vinegar. He lets this cook until the mixture will coat the back of the spoon, and then he adds the chicken pieces and mixes them thoroughly in the toffee-like juice.

113

Let people help themselves, after warning them that this is a hot peppery dish. West Indian cooks traditionally serve it with roast potatoes and coleslaw. I think the cole-slaw must be for the burnt-out mouths. It is a great compliment to be known for your rice and peas. Many West Indian men are excellent cooks, and very often the man of the family will bake all the bread and cakes.

When you have cooked this dish several times, you will soon adjust the seasoning to your taste. This is one of my favourite recipes.

Duck à l'Orange

There is nothing nicer than a crisply roasted duck with a strongly flavoured orange gravy. The problem is getting the gravy and the duck to absorb the orange flavour. The second problem is getting the skin crisp. If the duck is uncooperative, you can end up with greasy, flaccid lumps of flesh. I hang the duck off a hook in the kitchen for 24 hours. The idea is that the fat will run down the carcass; if you stick holes in the duck's nether regions, the fat should drip out on to the floor (thereby turning the kitchen into a skating rink for unwary visitors). This method does actually work. You can see the duck gradually losing its yellow fatty colour and turning a shade of grey. If, as so often happens to sluts, you forget, don't panic. Get out the hair-drier and stand there for half an hour blow-drying your duck. The only problem with this is that the neighbours will assume that it is the latest in way-out perversions.

1 duck (about 5¾ lb)	3 tablespoons red wine
Duck giblets	vinegar
2 onions	1 tin frozen orange juice
6 stalks celery	1 oz butter
4 carrots	4 oranges
½ pint duck stock	Salt and black pepper
3 tablespoons	to taste
granulated sugar	

get out the
hairdrier +
stand there FOR
½-hour BLOW-DRYING it

You can make the sauce beforehand. I do because I can't bear struggling with the duck and the gravy at the same time. Also, as it is a very fatty dish, the less time you have to spend hanging over the stove, the better. Simmer the giblets with the onions, celery and carrots for 2 hours. This will give you a rich tasty stock. If you don't have time, use a tin of chicken consommé. When the stock is ready, put the sugar into a saucepan and let it melt and bubble. Add the wine vinegar and let it evaporate until the mixture is like caramel. Pour in the stock and the orange juice. Let it simmer for a further half hour.

When you are ready to roast the duck, preheat the oven to 350° F, gas mark 3. Rub the bird all over with pepper, salt and flour. Stuff the cavity with two oranges cut into quarters.

Sit the duck on a trivet in a baking tray so that the fat can run freely. If you don't have anything resembling a trivet, and I certainly haven't, put it on the top shelf of the oven with a tray underneath. Cook the duck for 1½ hours, and then have a look at it. If you like it slightly underdone, the juice should run pink when you poke it. If you prefer it cooked right through, leave it until the juice is clear yellow. The bird should have crisp puffy skin and should be a warm brown colour. Strain the gravy out of the pan into the saucepan of giblets. While you are reheating the gravy, leave the duck in the hot oven with the door open and it will stay crisp.

Using a slotted spoon, lift out all the vegetables from the gravy and throw them away. Bring the gravy to the boil and stir it for a few minutes. Serve it separately from the duck, adding 2 oz of butter just before serving.

Carving a duck is always a problem. Use resident lover, who should have taken duck-carving lessons at the local tech. If you are up-market about this dish, you will serve it with home-made game chips and *petits pois*. I serve it with boiled potatoes or rice. It has such a strong flavour that vegetables are really wasted.

Pigeon Stew

If you are going to cook pigeons, you are well advised to

116

avoid the area of St James or, for that matter, any part of the country where pigeons gather in gangs and run the nation. Looking at their fierce little eyes and their scaly claws, it seems inconceivable that they should make an excellent casserole. Choose plump young pigeons from your butcher. Check the colour of their claws: they should be bright yellow. (Do remember to cut off their claws before you stew the birds. I once made a beautiful big casserole of pigeons in wine. Rather a lot of the wine went down my throat first, and I forgot to take the feet off. When I finally staggered to the table, I realized that all you could see was a forest of birds' feet sticking out of the dark brown gravy. Not a pretty sight, and no time to make jokes about psittacosis.)

6 pigeons	1½ bottles good
3 onions	Burgundy
6 large carrots	½ pint cream
½ lb streaky bacon	4 bay leaves
4 oz butter	Salt and pepper

Preheat oven to 325° F, gas mark 2.

Fill a bowl with water and a cup of vinegar. Immerse the pigeons and dry them thoroughly. If they still have claws, cut these off, and roll the birds in sufficient flour to give them a light coating. Heat the butter in a large casserole, and when it is foaming add the chopped onions and sliced carrots. Stir the vegetables round until the onions begin to brown.

Add the pigeons and make sure they are covered in the butter: keep turning them over for at least 10 minutes. Slowly pour in the Burgundy, and put the lid on tightly so that the wine does not evaporate. Cook in the oven for about 1½ hours. If the pigeons seem to be tough, the reason is that you have bought old ones; they will have to be cooked for a further 40 minutes. Pour the cream into the casserole just before serving.

Wild rice tastes excellent with this dish. If you serve wild rice, do remember to double the usual cooking time. Encourage people to use their fingers when getting to grips with the birds, otherwise guests unaccustomed to dismembering carcasses are liable to find the pigeons shooting across their plates.

Pheasant

Miss Williams, who had the onerous task of bringing me up, had many pheasants on her 250 acres of land. She was a great believer in hanging game until it was maggoty. She also believed that the feathers should be left on because they added taste to the bird as it decayed. I am sure she was right because they always tasted delicious. They had a sort of dark brown, slightly rotten taste. Those of us who are anally inclined will opt for hanging game for at least a week; Americans and other assorted squeamish guests would give tongue and refuse to eat the bird. The answer is to hang it and not tell anyone, unless you forget a maggot or two and they fall off someone's fork.

If the bird is 'well hung', the feathers will pull out easily. Don't hang your own game unless you know what you are doing and enjoy being up to your elbows in smelly conditions. Sluts rather like this sort of pastime: it makes them feel rural, but the cat goes A.W.O.L. until it's all over. If you don't have the time or the inclination, buy your pheasant from a good poultry shop and get someone to dress it for you. Do leave it for at least a couple of days out of the fridge if you buy it from a supermarket.

If your pheasant is young, consider roasting it as you would a chicken. Remember though that it is rather dry meat and benefits from being wrapped in bacon pieces while cooking. If the pheasants are older they will be tough, so it is a good idea to stew them in a rich sauce. They are far more likely to be old than young and tender. Most of the English countryside is leased out to mass murderers who go berserk in July and slaughter thousands of birds which are then rushed to restaurants all over Europe. Not many birds are left for the likes of you and me. You may be lucky and find a passing sporting lover who will supply you with fresh game, but you will have to be awfully fond of eating pheasant because that's the only kind of sport he'll have tiime for. Standing around in gum boots watching him shoot with his cronies is hardly a slut's idea of well-spent leisure, and English country houses are notoriously mean with their booze. (The sherry glass was an English middle-class invention to keep the guests from getting more than a mouthful of alcohol.)

3 pheasants (about 2½ lb each)	¾ pint chicken stock or consommé
12 shallots	¼ lb butter
½ lb streaky bacon	6 bay leaves
¾ lb mushrooms	Salt and black pepper to taste
6 large carrots	
½ bottle Madeira	

Preheat oven to 350° F, gas mark 3.

Melt the butter in a large casserole. Cut the bacon into 1-inch pieces and sweat them in the butter until the fat runs. Add the chopped shallots, sliced carrots and mushrooms, and stir them until the shallots begin to colour.

Dredge the pheasants in flour and put them into the casserole breast-side down, spooning the butter and vegetables over them. Add salt and freshly milled black pepper, and the bay leaves. Pour in the chicken stock and add the Madeira. Put the casserole into the oven and cook for 1 hour. Half way through, take the casserole out and turn the birds over.

I serve everyone with half a pheasant each. It does help to have a large pair of meat-cutters which you can simply run down the middle of each bird. Secateurs used for pruning roses will do. If they are rusty they will give your guests lockjaw. Sometimes, looking at the general state of British guests, this may not be a bad idea.

Boiled potatoes and a dish of Ratatouille (see p. 39) go well with this dish.

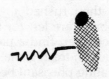

THREE
SALADS

Guests Like to have time to sit Round the Salad BOWL HAVING a Good Gossip

SALADS

Sluts love salads – all that lovely crisp fresh food with lots of herbs and garlic. Most people develop their own salad dressings, according to their particular likes and dislikes. I have never enjoyed the sharp taste of wine vinegar; I prefer to use a malt vinegar which makes a much gentler salad dressing. I hate salad dressings that pucker the mouth, and I do not like to have my salad dressing made with any oils other than olive, walnut or hazelnut.

Olive oil for salad dressing needs to be of the finest quality. You can argue all night over the merits of French or Italian oil, but I like the heavy, rich, dark green oil from Cyprus or Greece partly because I have such happy memories of my family in Zakinthos, and partly because I like the rich taste and smell. On the island, Mama Gina uses the first pressing of their olives to clean the babies and make salads; the rest of the pressings furnish the family and the taverna for everyday use. Walnut oil is heavily scented and quite delicious, as is hazelnut oil.

The Usual Slut's Salad Dressing

5 tablespoons olive oil	2 cloves garlic
2 tablespoons malt vinegar	Salt and freshly ground black pepper
1 teaspoon brown sugar	

Put the brown sugar into a small earthenware bowl. Using a garlic press, crush the garlic and stir it around with the

SLUtS LOVE SaLads
Because, Like CURRY
you caN Put aLMOSt
anyTHING INto them

sugar. Pour in the vinegar and mix with the garlic and sugar. Add the oil and then salt and pepper to taste. The brown sugar enhances and holds the taste of the other ingredients. From this basic dressing, I make all sorts of variations. A tablespoon of curry powder added to the dressing is delicious with a plain green salad. Different herbs completely transform a dull lettuce. Eight sprigs of apple mint cut into the dressing taste wonderful and fresh when added to the salad bowl.

Try these ideas for different salads. I serve a salad after the main course, which allows a pause before the already extended bellies of the guests are loaded with pudding or cheese. It is such a good way of cleansing the palate that I can't understand why people don't take salad more seriously in this country. It is a national disgrace that an English salad usually consists of a limp lettuce leaf upon which crouches a sulphurous egg. There is no other place in the world where one would be offered such an insult, and even the best English restaurants can rarely make a proper salad. I am sorry to say that even the American restaurant Surprise which boasted an American salad-bar was a disappointment. While I was lecturing in America, I was constantly delighted by the salad bars in hotels all across the continent.

Sluts love salads because they can, as with curry, put almost anything into them. The major snag about salads is that some people expect you to wash the lettuce. This is a mistake because unless you get the leaves bone-dry, the oil slips off and sits in a sullen pool at the bottom of the salad bowl. Low lights can hide a multitude of aphids. If you care about these things you can get one of those salad driers that work by centrifugal force, with a basket inside that whizzes round and round. The old method of putting the lettuce into a tea-towel and swinging it round one's head must have given British women peculiarly lopsided breasts. Sluts' tea-towels tend to be a rich reminder of months of glorious meals: if you use your tea-towels, you probably won't need a salad dressing. I usually buy three or four lettuces at a time and open them all up and put the leaves into the salad container in the fridge. The wildlife tends to prefer a warmer climate so it decamps, the slugs

IF YOU USE
YOUR TEATOWELS
YOU PROBABLY
WON'T NEED
A SALAD DRESSING

and the caterpillars bringing up the rear. This way I can have my lettuce crisp and fresh with only the odd lay-about worm remaining to provide a spot of extra protein.

You do need a large wooden salad bowl, but you don't necessarily have to have a fancy wooden fork and spoon to toss the salad, although wooden utensils tend to bruise the leaves less than metal ones. I lost my wooden set in a row with a neighbour. (She would have looked quite decorative, pinned to a tree with a salad fork through her heart, but I missed.) Anyway, I use my fingers, and the wooden bowl I have is nine years old. You should never wash a wooden bowl. Just wipe it out with a paper towel, and it builds layer upon layer of rich oils and herbs. I intend to have my salad bowl and garlic press buried with me just in case the Almighty isn't into salads.

Lettuces, like lovers, come in all shapes and sizes. My favourite is the Iceberg lettuce, but when they are not available in the shops, I buy the long green leafy cos lettuces from Cyprus or the huge endive lettuce that looks as though it's got an Afro hairstyle. English lettuces have a very delicate taste and are my favourite for serving if I want a plain green salad. I use two lettuces for a plain salad, and the basic salad dressing with a sprinkling of mint or tarragon.

Mixed Salad

1 large cos lettuce	1 green pepper
2 Spanish onions	1 red pepper
Watercress	¼ lb black olives
2 tomatoes	1 tin anchovies

Use the basic salad dressing. Break the lettuce leaves in two with your fingers – cutting the leaves just bruises them and they go black round the edges. Cut the onions into rings. If possible choose sweet mild onions that come from Spain or Greece, or use spring onions, remembering that the green stalks hold most of the taste.

Slice the tomatoes and peppers and layer them with the onions. Drain the tin of anchovies. If you don't like them too salty, put them in a saucer of milk for half an hour or so to drain the salt. Pat them dry with a paper towel. Chuck in the black olives and the watercress. This is a very pretty salad, the black sheen of the olives contrasting with the green and red of the peppers. You can make formal decorations with the ingredients if you wish, but sluts' salads tend to resemble the rest of their lifestyle and depend on chaotic inspiration.

If you can be bothered to fry some croutons, sprinkle them into the salad, for they give a lovely crunch to it and taste specially good if you fry them in bacon fat. Make them by cutting bread into tiny cubes and then frying the bits in a frying pan, turning them over a high heat until they go brown. In America, you can buy dozens of different sorts of croutons. The first enterprising person to educate the Great British public on the delights of multi-flavoured croutons in salads will make a lot of money.

Aubergine Salad

6 small aubergines
1 large Iceberg or cos
   lettuce
Basic salad dressing
   with 2 teaspoons of
   basil or origan added

3 tablespoons oil
Salt and pepper

Put the aubergines on a baking tray with the olive oil and bake them in a slow oven (325° F, gas mark 2) for 1 hour. By the end of an hour, you should be able to pierce them easily with a fork. Take them out and leave them to cool in the oil.

Just before you wish to make the salad, pour off the oil and lay the aubergines on a flat serving dish or on a bed of lettuce. Pour the dressing over the salad and add salt, basil or origan, and fresh black pepper to taste. Aubergines cooked this way have a very strong flavour and are quite filling, so I serve this dish after a fairly light main course and finish with cheese and fruit.

127

Green Bean Salad

1 English lettuce	6 slices streaky bacon
2 tins flageolet beans	Basic salad dressing

Drain the two tins of flageolet beans, put them into a salad bowl and mix them with the shredded lettuce. As you serve the main course, put the bacon under the grill and let it cook slowly until it is crisp and dry. Just before serving the salad, pour over the dressing and then crumble the bacon on to it. The beans and bacon complement each other very well indeed.

Potato Salad

The point of this salad is that it should be light. Most potato salads are heavy and weighed down with mayonnaise.

6 large waxy potatoes	¼ lb black olives
1 bunch watercress	1 cup basic dressing
1 bunch spring onions	

Boil the potatoes in their skins. When you can peel them easily, take off their skins. (This is much easier than peeling them beforehand, and it keeps the slices firmer.) Slice the potatoes fairly thinly. Put them to one side and chop the spring onions and watercress. Layer the watercress, onions and potatoes with the olives, stoned and halved. Pour the dressing over the salad. Do not toss it, as the potato slices are liable to disintegrate.

Leek Salad

This is such a pretty green salad. It looks beautiful on a white serving dish.

12 leeks	Basic salad dressing
2 large tomatoes	Parsley
4 tablespoons olive oil	Salt and black pepper
2 lemons	

Wash the leeks carefully. It is worth checking the top leaves to see that there is no sand between the layers because the salad will be ruined if it is all gritty. Put the leeks into a large saucepan with 4 tablespoons of olive oil and 2 tablespoons of water. Let the pan simmer with a tightly fitting lid for at least 30 minutes, and then check. The leeks should be firm, but you should be able to pierce the bulb easily with a fork. Take them off the stove and drain off the oil and water.

Let the leeks drain in a colander for about 15 minutes until they are quite dry. Squeeze the juice of a lemon over them while they are still warm. Put them on a large serving dish and pour the dressing over the salad. Place alternate wedges of lemon with slices of tomatoes on the top. Add salt and grind black pepper over it all, then sprinkle with parsley.

Spinach Salad

This is one of my favourite salads, as I love spinach.

2 lb young, fresh spinach leaves	Basic salad dressing
½ lb streaky bacon	Salt and pepper to taste

Only choose the freshest leaves. Discard the stalks and break the leaves in half with your fingers. Pour the dressing over the salad, and just before serving crumble the bacon into the salad bowl.

The recipes I have given here are just a few ideas for a salad break in the middle of a meal. There are endless varieties of salads that can be made up with any fresh or cooked vegetables. It is just a matter of using your imagination and of getting the confidence to try out any ideas you might have. I find that guests like to have time to sit round the salad bowl, having a good gossip while helping themselves with their fingers to bits and pieces. It's all very tribal, going back to the village cooking pot, which is how food should be eaten. I think it will take many years of retraining the British with regard to their eating habits before they get used to the idea that salads are a delicious course in their own right.

Loosen the salad in the bowl with a salad spoon. Peel the garlic and cut in two with a knife. Squeeze the juice with your fingers and discard the cloves. Do not brush with oil. Arrange the torn leaves in the salad bowl, then toss the bulb pieces of garlic. Take them out and discard the oil and garlic.

Cut the cheese into small pieces. Toss in a salad with very little oil. Squeeze the juice of a lemon onto the soft salt. Grind a pepper over it and toss over the dressing over the salad. Sprinkle with a little anchovy pieces or tomatoes, and top with salt and grind. Cut the cheese over and then sprinkle with parsley.

Spinach Salad

This recipe serves six, with whole anchovies.

	Butter
	oil and
	garlic

Chop/crush the washed leaves, and a clove of garlic leaves, to half with your fingers. Pour the dressing over the salad, and just before serving crumble the bacon into the salad bowl.

The proper thing to have given here, perhaps, is a few ideas for a salad break in the middle of a meal. There are endless varieties of salads that can be made up, with anything or cooked vegetables. It is just a matter of using your imagination and of eating the combinations to suit your tastes you might have. I feel that you should be free to have time to stand round the salad bowl mixing a good dressing with the various salads with them. Tomatoes, lettuce and cheese. It's all very artful going back to the village markets, for which is how food should be eaten. I think it will take many years of educating the British with regard to their eating habits but rather let most people see that salads are delicious dishes in their own right.

FOUR
PUDDINGS

a Good RICE PuddiNG caN BRiNG tEARS
to the eyes of the MOST HARdENED MeMBeRs
OF the RULING CLASS

PUDDINGS

You are either a pudding person or you're not. Sluts tend to have a few pudding recipes that they use from time to time, but they usually finish the meal with fruit and cheese. I notice that an awful lot of men get nostalgic for nursery food, though: a good rice pudding can bring tears to the eyes of the most hardened members of the ruling class. If you want to soften up a potential lover, check out his background. If he's from the East End, give him suet pudding or jam roly-poly. If he's from Eton, try apple crumble.

Everyone has an aunt who makes a special trifle. The old dear usually gets drunk on the sherry and falls into the bowl just as she is about to ladle it out. A good trifle is either a work of art or a graveyard of lumpy custard with hunks of dry cake sticking out.

Having people in your house for several hours is tiring enough in itself without working your fingers to the bone trying to put on a three-course meal. By the time your guests have finished the main course they are usually too drunk to care, and really just want to get into the coffee so they can pour themselves out of their chairs and into the car to go home. I find that many women get very competitive over who can produce the most lavish pudding. Very few people actually like eating gooey, cream-filled pastries after a big main course. But when the hostess spends the evening rabbiting on about how hard she has worked, it's difficult to refuse a dollop of the concoction. If it's summer, you may be able to flip it out of a window provided that your seat is strategically placed. Don't forget, you can

132

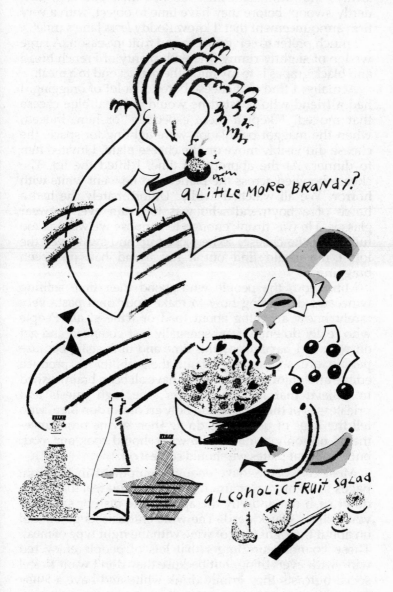

A LITTLE MORE BRANDY?

ALCOHOLIC FRUIT SALAD

always wait until someone's finished their pudding, then deftly swoop, before they have time to object, with a very firm announcement that 'I know Roddy *loves* Jane's trifle'.

I much prefer to serve cheese and fruit in season. A large wedge of slightly runny Brie with plenty of French bread and black grapes is to my mind the perfect end to a meal.

Actually, I find that cheese bores do a lot of bragging. I had a friend who boasted he would only eat blue cheese that moved. I kept a piece especially for him. Indeed, when the maggot population were fighting for space, the cheese did visibly move on the cheese plate. I invited him to dinner. At the appropriate time, I lifted the lid. The cheese boogied across the platter and he went white with horror. We all watched avidly. Unfortunately, he had a horse of a boyfriend who was too vain ever to wear glasses. He was drunk enough to suppose we were all too full to eat the cheese, so he picked up and swallowed the lot. I never did find out if my friend had just been bragging.

Mind you, the people who spend their time sniffing wine and discussing how to make your own pasta very rarely know anything about food or wine at all. People who really do enjoy food sensually just go ahead and get on with it. I have to say this time and time again because people are so insecure about their ability to produce edible and enjoyable meals. We have all been brainwashed to believe that it's the 'experts', the high priests and priestesses of the ancient and holy art of Cordon Bleu, who tell the likes of us how to do it. Their divine pronouncements not only command how we should cook our food, but also what plates we should serve it on.

Most cookbooks have enough equipment in the front pages to kit out a restaurant, and make you feel that if you don't rush out and buy the appropriate dish or saucepan you will be struck dead. The wine enthusiasts go on and on about the right type of wine with the right type of meal. These connoisseurs forget that lots of people enjoy red wine with everything, but because they don't want to feel social outcasts they grimly drink white and have a lousy evening.

Food, like most things in England, is riddled with class

taboos. Some people fall off their 'couch' clutching a beer, 'pissed as a newt', and are therefore presumed to live in Wigan. Others fall off their 'sofa' grasping a gin and tonic, 'half-cut', and are therefore supposed to live in Esher. The gin-and-tonic belt look down on the pie-and-mash brigade, and both sides deplore each other's taste in food. Sluts have a style of their own that transcends the class system with great ease – ease that causes the keepers of the war to suck their teeth in rage.

The following puddings are the few that I serve quite frequently. The amount of sugar I use may make these puddings much sweeter than you like: it's up to you to experiment, rather than slavishly following the directions of yet another cookbook. The whole point of cookbooks should be to encourage people to develop their own creativity. For far too long, the experts have poured out a never-ending stream of complicated directions, making most of us feel horribly inadequate as soon as we go near our kitchens.

Make a point of checking out your local delicatessen. Adamou's is always importing things like excellent jars of figs and preserved cherries from all over the world. They are marvellous as puddings as you just decant them and serve.

Brandy Snaps and Cream

I love brandy snaps – especially the ones that come airtight in tins, because I would not dream of making them.

> 12 brandy snaps (or more
> if the main course is light)
> 1 pint double cream

Just before serving the brandy snaps, pour cream over them. Or you can whip the cream until it is really thick and then spoon it into the hollow roll. If the cream doesn't thicken just to spite you, add a squeeze of lemon juice and it will thicken immediately.

Alcoholic Fruit Salad

The booze for fruit salad depends on you. I add brandy. Other people like various liqueurs or white wine. If you're feeling extravagant, try all sorts of mixtures. White wine and Grand Marnier taste good together. Also try kirsch, which tastes of almonds but is made from cherries. Curaçao is good with slices of oranges to complement its orange flavour.

I once spent a delightful weekend by myself with a dozen miniature bottles of various liqueurs and some good dry white wine, making up mixtures and sloshing them on to piles of chopped-up fruit. I wish I could give you the recipe that emerged from forty-eight hours of total concentration. Unfortunately, like most of the fruits of one's most brilliant and inspired moments, the recipe got lost in the mist of alcohol fumes. (Perhaps that is why most Nobel prizewinners and famous scientists are teetollers.) By Monday morning, I had a wet towel round my head and was swearing I'd never do it again. At least not until the next time.

1 large bunch black grapes	2 large Chinese gooseberries
1 large bunch white grapes	2 tablespoons caster sugar
3 large bananas	¼ bottle brandy
2 oranges	¼ bottle white wine
1 lemon	

Posh people peel their grapes. It takes hours and the juice runs down your elbows. If you can't get seedless grapes you have to decide whether you have the kind of guests who are uninhibited enough to spit the seeds out like short bursts of gun-fire, or whether they are the sort who hint darkly at stoppages of the bowel and appendicitis. A quick description of the examination necessary to verify an attack of appendicitis is usually enough to stop the conversation dead in its tracks. However, if you are the sort who is a 'true Christian martyr', you will go ahead anyway and spend hours skinning and depipping the grapes.

Sluts cut the grapes in half and put them in a large bowl. Glass bowls look lovely full of a multi-coloured fruit salad. Trendies like to use chamber pots for effect. If you don't have a fruit bowl, you can usually find a pretty Victorian pudding bowl at a local junk shop.

Slice the bananas into the bowl. Choose the bananas that are very yellow and quite soft so that they are sweet and will absorb the alcohol. Peel the oranges and the lemon and slice them very thinly, then add them to the rest of the fruit. Look out for Chinese gooseberries: they look like furry chipolata sausages and don't taste of much, but they are a lovely sensitive shade of green when layered on the top of the fruit salad.

Sprinkle 2 tablespoons of caster sugar over the lot. Add the brandy and dry white wine, and leave it all to mellow on a ledge somewhere. (Make sure the ledge is a high one, or else the cats will later be seen to stagger about in a highly undignified manner.) If you are making the salad the night before, put it in the fridge, but if it only has a few hours to marinate, leave it outside. You can serve the fruit salad with warm cream, but this does make it very rich.

Plums in Brandy

You need a large wide-mouthed jar with an air-tight lid. It is worth making a large amount at any one time as it has to sit for three months. The problem with this recipe is having that much brandy sitting in the house for that amount of time. When funds are low and the prospect of drinking water looms ahead, it is tempting to syphon off the brandy. The answer for weak-willed sluts like myself is to put the jar in the safe keeping of the vault – you'll find the bank manager will be very obliging, especially if you promise him a taste.

These quantities will feed six people, and leave enough left over to make it worth while.

3 lb Victoria plums	4 tablespoons water
(not too ripe)	Enough brandy to cover
4 tablespoons sugar	the plums

Before everyone panics at the cost of the brandy, remember that this is an incredibly rich pudding, so this amount of plums will see you through at least enough people to make the cost less than exorbitant.

I hope you do not expect me to remind you to wash the plums and remove the stalks. I mention this only because most recipe books treat their readers like cretins. Sluts never wash anything, and you are either the sort of person who washes things or you aren't, in which case there is no point in reminding you because you won't do it anyway.

Prick all the plums with a fork so that the juices will run into the brandy. Put the sugar and water into a saucepan and boil it on a high heat until it coats the back of a spoon. In case you haven't tried it before, that is exactly what happens. The syrup starts to get thicker as the water boils away, and the mixture sticks to the spoon. It is then ready to be poured into the jar.

Put the plums in and fill the jar to the brim with brandy. Seal the top and put it away for three months. When you get it out again and take off the lid, a lovely rich smell of brandy mixed with the summer odour of plums will invade the room. You can serve it with cream, and you should keep the jar in the kitchen or the guests will try and get through the lot. It's a nice pudding to make in September for Christmas.

Summer Fruit and Kirsch

This is a very similar recipe to the one above. It depends on the fruit of the season. Raspberries, gooseberries, strawberries – the list is endless. Just layer the fruit with a sprinkling of caster sugar on the top and then add half a bottle of dry white wine and one teacup of kirsch.

Apple and Mint Fruit Salad

8 apples (Granny Smiths   8 sprigs apple mint
    are good)
½ bottle dry cider

Peel and core the apples. Slice them very thinly into a bowl filled with water to which you have added the juice of a lemon, in order to stop the slices from going brown. When you are ready to put the fruit salad together, remove the apples gently. Chop the mint very coarsely and add it, a few pinches at a time, as you layer the apples so that the mint taste permeates the dish. Pour over the cider and chill until ready to serve.

Baked Apples

This is a very easy dish. You can add all sorts of spices and fillings, or you can simply core the apples, cook them and serve them with cream.

6 large baking apples	6 heaped teaspoons
6 teaspoons honey	chopped almonds
2 oz butter	¼ bottle cider

Most people like baked apples and it's easy to prepare and cook them while the guests are ploughing their way through the main course. You can also bake the apples the day before and serve them cold if you want to make the meal even more relaxed.

Preheat oven to 325° F, gas mark 3.

Core the apples. There are such things as apple-corers, but they never work for me. They are designed for the apple that has its core in the right place. Like belly buttons, every apple core seems to have a mind of its own, and the instrument usually digs out half and leaves a horrible crater. I use a potato peeler if I have to do it myself. If possible, I get someone else to do it so I can scream at them if they get it wrong. Cut the apples round the middle with a sharp knife – they have a horrible habit of exploding if you don't remember to do this – and sit them all in a shallow baking dish.

Mix the nuts with the honey and stuff the mixture into the gaping holes. Melt the butter in a small saucepan and pour it over the apples so that they are coated. Then pour the cider round them and put them into the oven. Cook for 1 hour or more, depending on their size. When you can push a fork straight through them, they are ready. Serve them with thick fresh cream.

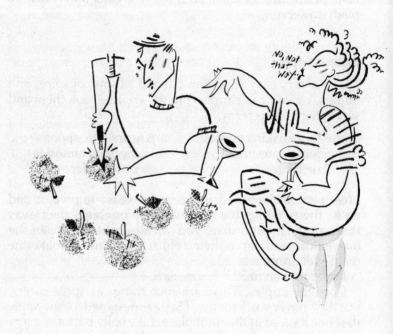

I USE a Potato PeeLer
IF POSSIBLE I GeT SomeoNe ELse
to Do iT So I CAN SCREAM aT
them iF they GeT iT WRONG

Sugar Daddy's Favourite Pudding

How to feed men is the subject of another book, but this is one of those nourishing dishes that is always a success.

1 lb raspberries	¼ lb sugar
½ lb red currants	1 loaf white bread

I use a pudding basin or a soufflé dish if I can find one that isn't broken. Line the dish with one-day-old white bread with the crust cut off. Use a sandwich loaf to get the right thickness. Make sure that you make the lining as leak-proof as possible so that no juice escapes.

Put the sugar and berries into a saucepan and cook for 4 minutes (just so that their juice runs into the sugar). Put the fruit aside to cool, then spoon it into the dish, leaving aside a little of the juice for serving.

Cover the top of the fruit with a tightly fitting layer of bread, and put a plate over it. Find a 3 lb weight and stick it on top of the plate. Leave it overnight in the fridge. When you are ready to serve it, turn it out on to a dish and pour over the reserved juice. If the fruit is out of season, check a large Marks and Spencer's, because they usually have very good frozen fruits.

Peaches in Red Wine

Another dish to serve hot or cold. I serve almost everything to do with puddings cold if I can, because I make them (when I remember) well in advance. Also, it's no strain during the meal this way. I notice so many hostesses looking like spaniels, head to one side and an ear cocked for the sound of a buzzer from the kitchen. After twenty years of giving dinner parties, this posture becomes permanent.

6 large peaches	6 tablespoons sugar
1 bottle good red wine (Beaujolais)	

Peel the peaches and put them into a large casserole. Sprinkle the sugar over them. Pour in the bottle of wine and bring it to boiling point. When it is just bubbling, turn it down to simmer. Let the wine just shiver and cook slowly for 1 hour, turning the peaches over after 30 minutes, so that they are evenly cooked. They should be red from the wine.

If I am going to serve this dish cold, I make it the day before and put it in the fridge. When it is cold, the syrup is thick and the peaches are a wonderful colour. I serve it with thick cream. If you are in a hurry, you can just slice fresh peaches into wine glasses, add a teaspoon of sugar to each glass, and pour the wine over the fruit.

Stewed Plums

Plums can be very boring, but they too taste good in wine.

1½ lb Victoria plums (or any good cooking plum)	5 tablespoons brown sugar
	1 bottle good Beaujolais

Preheat oven to 325° F, gas mark 3.

Prick the plums and put them into a large pie dish. Sprinkle them with the sugar and add the wine, and put them in the oven. After about an hour have a look at the dish, and if the plums are soft but still holding their shape, they are ready. Serve hot or cold.

Upside-down Apple Pie

This is a little more elaborate but fun to make.

6 large cooking apples (or more, depending on the size of your casserole)	6 tablespoons water
	1 packet shortcrust pastry
6 heaped tablespoons sugar	

Peel and cut the apples into quarters, and leave them in a bowl of water with the juice of a lemon added while you make the syrup. Boil the sugar and water fast in a casserole until it begins to thicken. Add the quartered apples, standing them upright like soldiers and packing the dish so that they can't fall over. Put a very tight lid on the casserole and simmer as slowly as you can for 1 hour. After an hour, do not lift the lid, just put the casserole aside to go cold, and put it in the fridge overnight.

The next morning, preheat the oven to 450° F, gas mark 8. Roll out the pastry as you would for a pie, and put it over the apples in the casserole. They should still be intact. If they aren't, you cooked them too fast, and you will have to pretend you always meant to serve apple sauce. If all is well, put the dish into the oven to cook the pie crust. When it has cooled put it back in the fridge.

To serve, take a knife that you have heated on the stove and run it round the pie, loosening the crust from the sides. Turn the casserole upside-down on to a flat serving dish. The apples should have caramelized with the syrup, and it will taste delicious. Serve it with cream.

Erin's Favourite Pudding

This recipe is for two people. However, if you are Japanese, adjust the catering and the bathing facilities to suit your needs.

> 1 bottle Dom Perignon champagne (or your favourite
>   bottle of anything; I know someone who swears by
>   VP Cherry Wine)
> 2 large ripe peaches
> 1 bottle Femme bath oil
> 1 hot bath

I assume you are intelligent enough to work out the logistics of this recipe.

The list of possible puddings is endless. But sluts tend to stick to simple dishes because puddings and cakes take time and effort. I have never known a slut who can make a cake or produce anything vaguely resembling a soufflé. In my early youth I tried to compete with my peers, and would agonize over my failure to get anything to rise. My efforts at cake-making produced inedible lumps of concrete. I used to make my children's birthday cakes out of packets; I felt horribly guilty about this so I kept it a secret. Looking back, I remember trying to make all sorts of puddings, only to be forced to throw them out as they wobbled and collapsed. It was a long time before I decided that it wasn't that I was a horribly bad cook, nor was I a failure as a woman. I just did not have the talent required to produce beautiful pastry. At the same time I realized that I didn't really like most puddings and pastries. The recipes above are the few that I enjoy and use.

ERIN'S FAVOURITE PUDDING

The following are ones that I *don't* use, but believe it or not they are genuine: three gruesome recipes from Malaysia, Singapore and Saudi Arabia respectively. It is hard to imagine them giving enjoyment to anyone, though they presumably must.

Monkey's Brains

I must point out that custom did not allow any woman to come to the table during the serving of this course. I believe it is now banned by law, but is still practised privately. The table has a round hole in the middle. After the guests are seated, each clutching a teaspoon, a small boy runs under the table holding a monkey. The host slices off the top of the monkey's head, exposing the brain. The guests immediately help themselves with their teaspoons.

Duck's Feet

Unfortunately, I was served this dish at a Chinese feast some years ago in Singapore. Ducks are kept in cages specially designed with slatted floors. The ducks' legs hang down through the slats so that the feet never touch the ground. When the time comes, the feet are chopped off and are then poached in a sauce of soy and ginger. They are served about four to a bowl and taste awful.

Sheep's Eyes

I was offered an eye in a Bedouin tent as a mark of honour. The only thing to do was to take it, pretend it was a marble, stick it in my mouth and swallow hard. It went down and didn't come up again. I can't describe the cooking method, as I had my eyes shut for most of the meal.

Enough of exotica.

Thank God there is a healthy movement afoot to liberate us from the slavery of cooking. It was ten years ago that Katharine Whitehorn absolved us from the guilt-ridden religion of housework, and it has taken all this time to extend that absolution wholeheartedly to meals. In fact, the meals shared by members of a family or by friends should be cheerful times, not silent battles or competitions.

145

Contraception gave women the freedom to enjoy sex without the fear of pregnancy; convenience food should give her the added freedom of hours that used to be spent slaving in the kitchen over a hot stove. These days anyone can follow the instructions on a packet and, with a little imagination, provide an interesting meal. Blood, sweat and tears have no place at the table. If you have a mother-in-law who has dominated your partner's life with her home-cooking, then retrain your partner. He won't starve and will soon realize that home-cooking often comes with such a heavy measure of guilt that a tin of beans and a happy smile are preferable to the sight of the women in his life tottering around the kitchen, muttering the equivalents of 'Oy vay'.

Don't force your children to eat your carefully prepared home-made stews when what they really want is fish fingers and beans (which are just as nutritious anyway). Do teach your kids and your partners to cook for themselves. Any ten-year-old should be able to put together a plate of food that will keep them all quiet for the evening if you don't feel like cooking. Remember that kids get addicted to hamburgers for years of their lives. They don't like them home-made; they like them from the take-away, so don't whine – get them a take-away when you can afford it. When you can't, let them choose what they want to eat. It's an amazing medical fact that if you leave children alone, they will choose a fairly balanced diet for themselves.

I often feel that the whole ritual of the evening spent agonizing in the kitchen followed by the serving of a complicated meal appeals mainly to women who don't enjoy sex. By the time the washing-up is over, they can legitimately announce that they are tired and have a headache. I have never known a really happy, sensuous woman who has made a fetish out of serving food. Ladies who throw highly organized dinner parties with lots of courses are, in my experience, usually uptight and neurotic. Their food is usually beautifully presented but tasteless, and you could never imagine them in bed with anyone because any thrashing about would disturb their elaborate hairstyles.

As a nation, we spend very little on food compared with

our European counterparts. Maybe the time has come for us to reintroduce food and pleasure at our tables. Most Continental countries have endless sausages, salamis, pâtès and other delicacies to whet the appetite. We have an extraordinarily arid history of food. Even our family life doesn't include the long hours spent round the table in other countries. Now that producing a meal can be so much easier for us than it was for our mothers, maybe we can use that time to sit with glasses of wine and plates of food, feeling the pleasure of sharing time with family and friends. Sluts do it. So what if the kitchen is a mess? If you don't want to wash up, use paper plates and cups. If you don't feel like cooking, Marks and Spencer run an excellent line of different kinds of ready-to-cook dishes. As long as it tastes good, the guests don't mind who made it.

Next time you invite people to your house to eat, think about yourself first. Forget the years of training that decree that in order to produce a meal you must suffer and make others suffer. If you don't like cooking, don't cook. You can perfectly well feed people with pâté, French bread and a salad. The end of a meal should leave you tucked up in bed with a happy smile on your face. Life is too short to spend a large part of it over a hot stove.

Sluts never apologize, because they feel responsible for themselves, not for other people. If someone doesn't like a slut's food or her house or her way of dressing, she feels it's their problem, not hers. In fact, she will probably feel a little sorry for them because sluts have kind hearts. She watches television advertisements with amusement, secure in the knowledge that the women in the ads have nothing to do with her life.

She is also aware that those women who follow the dictates of fashion are furiously jealous of her. After all, they work their fingers to the bone producing exquisite food; they spend years reading the latest books and going to the cinema so that they will be scintilating company; they spend more than they can afford on a little black dress or a label that will immediately identify the price tag. If they are unattached, they feel amputated. If they are attached, they are usually very unkind to their partners. In short, they have no identity of their own. They are hollow shells inside which the small, unique girl-child gave up and died years ago.

Sometimes the girl-child can come back to life. Instead of being furiously jealous of the slut's easy-going lifestyle, a woman may take another look and like what she sees. Out go the books on cooking that make her feel inadequate. Out go the torturous clothes and shoes. Out go the people whose competitive natures pushed her further and further away from herself.

She is at last open enough to live as *she* pleases. Her life takes on a new glow. She puts her feet up with a glass of wine and lets the world struggle by. Nothing upsets her except people who are unkind to each other. But the sight of fresh field mushrooms or of a beautiful piece of beef puts it all into perspective. The lifestyle of a slut is indeed a happy one.

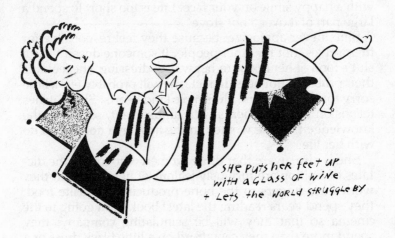

SHE PUTS HER FEET UP
WITH A GLASS OF WINE
+ LETS THE WORLD STRUGGLE BY

INDEX

149

151

CROCKPOT COOKING

Mary Norwak

The Crockpot – the revolutionary combination of traditional
cooking methods and modern technology . . . an
earthenware casserole which you just switch on before
leaving for work. It cooks gently all day, using only the
power needed for an electric light bulb. And you come
home to a perfectly-cooked meal.

Our ancestors knew the value of leaving their stews to cook
gently for hours in an earthenware pot – and, with the
crockpot, we can enjoy the same delights despite the
restrictions of a working day. The crockpot is economical,
safe – there's no danger of boiling over, burning or cooking
dry – and it preserves the flavours and nutritional values of
foods.

Bestselling cookery author Mary Norwak tells you all you
need to know about crockpots – how to use and look after
them, the best cooking methods for various foods and, of
course, dozens of delicious recipes from soups, stews and
fish, to jams and pickles.

Futura
Cookery
0 8600 7579 6

All Futura Books are available at your bookshop or newsagent, or can be ordered from the following address:
Futura Books, Cash Sales Department,
P.O. Box 11, Falmouth, Cornwall.

Please send cheque or postal order (no currency), and allow 45p for postage and packing for the first book plus 20p for the second book and 14p for each additional book ordered up to a maximum charge of £1.63 in U.K.

Customers in Eire and B.F.P.O. please allow 45p for the first book, 20p for the second book plus 14p per copy for the next 7 books, thereafter 8p per book.

Overseas customers please allow 75p for postage and packing for the first book and 21p per copy for each additional book.